Visible Confidence

7 Steps to Life and Career Changing Confidence

Chantelle Anderson

Visible Confidence
7 Steps to Life and Career Changing Confidence

To you, so you'll never feel like less than enough.
And to Kristin, for your unwavering belief in me
and my dreams.

CONTENTS

PROLOGUE
(Read this anyway)

This book isn't going to be full of clinical advice. If you're expecting a collection of proven research and big words then please stop reading... I'd hate to disappoint you.

I wrote this book because I know what it's like to feel like nothing, and I want you to know that you should never feel like less than enough.

Or maybe you don't feel like nothing, but too often you stand there, knowing there's something you should do, or were even meant to do, but for whatever reason you don't believe you can. I've been there too.

Wherever you are in your confidence journey, I wrote this for you.

Also, since this book felt like "girl talk" to me, I used feminine pronouns most of the time. Guys, I still love you! The great thing is, these principles 100% apply to you too. So if you're reading this, THANKS, and just switch things up when needed.

Visible Confidence

7 Steps to Life and Career Changing Confidence

Introduction
FIRST THINGS FIRST

*"If there's any definition to being perfect,
you're perfect at being yourself."* ~ Zendaya

Is confidence a feeling?

It can be. But feelings come and go, and we'd kind of like confidence that stays, right? That brand of confidence – the staying kind – is more a state of being that when genuine, is impossible to hide from others.

I call it Visible Confidence. And since we're going to be talking about it for the rest of this book, we need to know what it means.

Visible Confidence is never flashy but is immediately noticeable. It doesn't come off with anything you can take off.

Everyone sees it, but those who equate worth with status, wealth or appearance will never truly understand it.

Visible confidence starts inside us and touches every part of our bodies before spilling out onto those around us.

So how do we get it? For the longest time, I had no idea!

I haven't always been the person in the picture on the cover of this book. Even now, sometimes I don't feel like her. Here's the girl I remember:

I showed these pictures to my friend, Lee, the other day and she was like, "Wow, thank God…just thank Him," as she laughed hysterically. Ha, thanks girl.

The journey from that girl to the woman on the cover may or may not shock you, but it blows my mind every time I think about it! Still, even along the way, no matter how high I climbed on my own to-do list, for the longest time one thing was always missing. That one thing was confidence.

I'm guessing that at some point, you've felt how I used to feel:

I want to do great things but I'm not sure if I'm good enough to make great happen.
I have something to say, but what if it doesn't come out right?
I wish I could believe what other people say about me.
Can I trust myself enough to follow my heart?
I just want the person I show people and the person I feel like to be the same person!
How do I turn off these voices in my head telling me I can't do it?
I just don't feel pretty…

Thoughts like these aren't unusual; they're actually totally normal. We all need more confidence in one area or another. But there's always that one thought stalking everything we do:

Am I enough?

I think this question is engraved on our brains no matter who we are. It seems like some people can answer, "Yes!" as soon as they can speak, while others of us take a little – or a lot – longer to realize that we just might be. Yes, I am definitely in that latter group and if you're reading this, maybe you are too.

Of course it doesn't help when everything around us is saying, "You'll be so much better if you get that guy or become more stylish or get your boobs done or get your dream career." That's what they want you to believe. "They" being the people selling the magazines or the guys or the plastic surgeons (laughing). But the TRUTH is that you are enough without any of that outside validation. No additions…no gimmicks…just you!

I'm not saying be satisfied with where you are. I know the superhero in you would never allow that! But WHERE you are and WHAT you are, are totally different than WHO you are.

Try this: Make a list of all the good things about yourself. Literally, right now! Write down as many as you can think of. Next to each item on your list, write down the reason it's a good thing.

For example: I've always been curious. That's a good thing because the more questions you ask, the more you learn.

I call it my, "I Am" list. It's cool because when you're done you'll have a list of positives about yourself that you can learn to recognize and appreciate more. That's the first step to Visible Confidence.

You have everything you need to get everything you need.

I understand you might not believe you're enough yet. That's totally ok because confidence isn't found; it's built. Building your own confidence is one of the most influential things you'll ever do. But you have to be willing to put in the time and do the work, and that's why you're here so great already! I know it's possible to go from shy and questioning to outspoken and confident because I've done it.

So this book is everything that's helped me, and that I still use on a regular basis to live confidently. And I'm going to be completely honest about my mess-ups, struggles and the journey itself because that's the only thing that's going to help any of us.

Super excited to go on this journey with you. So lets get started!

Step 1
CHASE FEAR AND WIN!

"Confidence doesn't mean you don't have insecurities.
Confidence is taking action despite those insecurities."

Has there ever been a time when fear got the best of you?

I remember during my freshman year of college, I was super shy, and so my basketball coach made me take a public speaking class to get over it. I was terrified.

The day of my first speech my stomach felt like I'd spent the last eight hours on a rollercoaster. I remember walking to class with note cards in my sweaty hands and peeking through the window on the door. When I saw my audience, I walked right back to my dorm room. Totally skipped the class!

I definitely lost that fight!

But it's always the same. Fear tells us that we won't be good enough at whatever we're trying to do. And because we're not good enough, of course we're going to fail at it. And when we fail, everyone will know we failed, and no one likes a failure, right? So then we won't have any friends and without friends, we won't fall in love, and if we don't fall in love, we'll never be happy. And of course it all started from trying to do something we weren't good enough to be good at anyway. Right?

Ok, maybe that's just my inner monologue sometimes, but I doubt it. Our minds can really run away with us if we let them. When that happens I've trained myself to say, "Really Chantelle? Stop it!"

Win the fight.

Think of the last thing you were scared to do but did anyway. Like really picture it.

Maybe you talked to someone you were intimidated by and they ended up being really cool, or spoke in front of a group and did better than expected. Maybe you went on a trip somewhere new and had a blast. You can probably look back now and laugh at yourself for being scared. And that's my point. Sometimes you just have to tell that little voice in your head to "Shut up!" and do it anyway.

The most important fights you'll ever win are in defending yourself from your own doubts.

For me, one of them was writing this book. I wasn't scared of the actual writing; I love that part. But I was scared that when I gave people the option to buy it, they wouldn't. Or worse, they'd buy it and hate it. My decision to keep writing with the intention of letting you read it was an ongoing argument with that little whisper saying, "You can't do it."

But that's what Fear does. It tells you it's better to do nothing because anything you do won't be good enough.

And then you have to ask, "Good enough for who?"
Usually Fear will say something like, "people."
Then you have to ask yourself, who are these people I'm so worried about not being good enough for?
Do they have names?
And what have they done to earn my concern?
I ask myself these questions all the time! In most cases, "people" is a term used by Fear to describe an ambiguous group that has no effect on your life one way or the other. Even if they do have names and faces, if they don't support you in trying to be better, do they really deserve to have that influence over your thoughts and actions? No, they don't. Not at all.
When the voice of Fear starts feeding you unproductive thoughts about who you are or what you're doing, fight it with the right questions.

FACT: No one is born without fear.

Fearlessness is impossible. Saying be fearless is just like saying be perfect. It's just not going to happen no matter how hard we try. And God knows that we try!
The most successful, invincible person you know is afraid sometimes. The difference between them and everyone else is that they argue with Fear and win those arguments more often than not. What we all see is the result after the struggle, not the battle they won to get there.
In telling ourselves to be fearless we're setting ourselves up for failure. It's conditioning our minds to believe there's something wrong with us for being scared. But that's not true at all.
Instead of trying not to feel fear we need to learn how to handle it. Other-

wise when it does show up we're going to freak out because we're not going to expect it and be like, "Oh my gosh, I'm scared, what do I do?"

And really, we don't need to just acknowledge fear. We need to chase it because Fear hangs out with anything worth doing!

Seriously, Fear is awesome because there's no progress without it. The fact that we're scared means we're going somewhere new, doing something new or growing in some way. That's a great thing!

Chasing fear makes us embrace the opportunity that comes with it. Embrace the opportunity meaning welcome the chance to be courageous. With- out fear there is no courage.

So if you're sitting there saying, "Yeah, I'm fearless," then you're short-changing yourself. You're discounting the courage it takes to push those fears aside and go get what you want.

It's so funny when I meet people they assume that I'm just this fearless person, and trust me I correct them very quickly. Because the truth is, I'm scared of a lot!

I remember when I first went to play pro basketball overseas after college. I was leaving to go over there for 7 months and balled my eyes out for the first 30 minutes of the 8-hour flight to Hungary. 6'6" and 22-years-old, still crying like a baby! I was so scared.

But after having overcome the fear of going and figuring things out – which wasn't always easy but I did it – the next time I had to go, even though I was nervous, I wasn't afraid. Since then, I've traveled and lived all over the world.

Now getting on a plane to go anywhere is the same as getting in the car and driving to work, except way more exciting and I need more luggage. I would've missed so many amazing opportunities and experiences by staying home on account of fear.

It's not that I'm special. Not at all. That's just how confronting fear works. You earn your own confidence little by little in doing what you're scared of until the fear goes away. Everything you dream of is hidden behind every-thing you're afraid of. And it's not going to just move; you have to push it out of the way!

As you do that, your fear OF doing will become confidence IN doing. It's like building a resume in your mind that you can refer to as you go along. When I'm questioning myself, I think of the last time I succeeded at some-thing I thought was going to be hard, or did something I was afraid of.

Like when I was in medical sales, I would get anxious walking into a big account because I hadn't been successful there before. Then I reminded myself how my last big deal started the same way, with me walking into an account I'd never done business with.

Just like that, my previous victory over fear helped me beat it again. Your job is to keep building that resume so you have more and more references. Then like all good references, use them!

Even once we've built up our confidence, we're going to have times when we don't feel or act confident. Feelings have a special way of making you feel fragile, no matter how strong you are. That's why it's so important to have systems in place to help you maintain what you've built.

I call it my Confidence Kit, and we're going to be putting together throughout this book. I use it most often when I'm scared but really, you can use it any time you don't feel confident.

THE CONFIDENCE KIT

Fear Resume – We just talked about this one. Every time you're scared of something, do it anyway, and it turns out well, file that away in your Fear Resume. Make a list on your phone or put one in your wallet that you can refer to when you doubt yourself. It will redirect your focus from your fear to your success.

Pep Talk Person – We all need that one person who will not only give us a pep talk when needed, but also 100% believes every word they're telling us. I have two people in particular who I know I can go to for this and they are priceless. Sometimes we need someone to believe in us during the moments we don't.

"You can do it" Playlist – How awesome is music? It can change how we're feeling at any given moment. That's why it's important to have a playlist of songs that make you feel invincible. Sometimes I'll put one song on repeat for as long as it takes me believe whatever it's saying. When you don't have a pep talk person around, or you don't want to bug them for the third time that week, it's a great substitute!

Positive Scriptures and Quotes – Sometimes there's nothing better than a quote that says exactly what you need to hear at exactly the right time. I have a quote book where I keep all of my favorite and most classic words of wisdom. I'd recommend it to anyone. Also, when I'm questioning whether I can do something or not, I always read scriptures about God's promises for my life. I actually made a bookmarked list using the Bible app on my phone and named it "Promises." If you have a strong faith or even want to grow in yours, this is a great practical. Some of my faves are Isaiah 41:13, 1 Corinthians 2:9, and Psalm 145:17-19. Think of it as your "You can do it playlist," but in the Bible. Gives me confidence every time!

"I Am" List and Evidence Pictures – We already talked about the "I Am" list and we'll go over evidence pictures later. Just know that when your feelings are lying to you by telling you you're not good enough, you need to confront their lies with evidence. Take the list of your great qualities we made earlier and put it in your phone. Look at it during those times when your feelings distract you from your awesomeness. And when you find your evidence picture, even if it's just one, don't be afraid to use that too! It's the easiest way to make the voices in your head play nice until you can change their minds.

One more thing: Don't let pointless things be the only time you beat fear. I mean, it's cool to go on a rollercoaster or skydive. But make sure you're not only using your courage for experiences that get you nowhere. Win the fight for something that matters and use that decision to help you move forward.

A while back, people coined the term, "YOLO." I hated it even back then, but it stood for, "You Only Live Once." Which is true. But people were using it as an excuse to do dumb stuff that benefitted them nothing and got them nowhere.

Wanna get super drunk tonight? YOLO.

Wanna have sex with that hot guy or girl you just met? YOLO.

Wanna drop a few grand on a vacation you can't afford? YOLO.

At first thought, you might agree with the whole, "Let's have as much fun as we can because this life is our only chance" mindset. But this is also our only chance to dream huge, create the life we want and become people who impact others in a positive way. So let's not sacrifice the substance for the fun. **Fun comes after the work, with your dreams.** Spend your courage wisely. If you're going to jump, get something for it that will last!

Hold on though…

Now that you're hopefully excited to get out there and try new things, hold on a second. Because I don't want you to go all buck wild and then be like, "Well Chantelle told me to." There's a decision process that needs to happen in front of every "Just Do It!"

So, if it's an on the fly decision, ask yourself:

Will this kill me, injure me or put me in jail?

If the answer is "yes" or "maybe", it's probably not a good idea. Sometimes we want to do things for the excitement of it. I totally get that. In fact, I'm thankful I don't have scars or a record for the amount of times I failed to ask this question. Fun is great. Just try to make sure it won't have lasting consequences afterwards.

Is it sexual in nature? Yes?

If there's a question about whether to do it or not, the answer should probably be no. Sexual stuff is in a completely different category in that it can't be fixed but only healed from. Plus, if you say no and regret it afterwards, trust me when I say you can almost always change that "no" to a "yes" later. Some opportunities only knock once, but sex is not one of them. On the other hand, if you say "yes" and regret it afterwards, there's nothing you can do to change your mind or the situation. I've never said "no" and wished I had said "yes". But it has definitely gone the other way around. Just be smart.

Does it fit with who I am?

If the answer is yes, go for it! I ask myself this question all the time. My mind will say, "But what will they think?" And I'll say, "Who cares, it's me!" We need to quit the habit of letting other people's perceived thoughts dictate our lives. What I've found is that usually, they don't end up thinking what we think they'll think. That's a lot of thinking to be replaced with doing!

Then there's that thing that's been on your heart forever, stalking your thoughts. That dream career or big idea. It's never going to leave you alone until you stop thinking, "What if I fail," and just do it anyway.

Here's your To Do List:

Google it. Get preliminary information. Do you really want to do it?

Really research it. Google isn't enough. Find books and other resources to help you look at it from every angle. Talk to people with experience AND success in that area. If you don't know any of those people, find them.

Pray about it. If this is your thing, do it often.

Count the cost. What could get in your way? Are you really prepared to do whatever it takes to make it happen? This step is key. If you move forward without it, you risk starting and having to stop halfway through. That will definitely cue the inner monologue on failure we talked about earlier.

Get the materials together. Build your team if you need one.

AFTER you've done all of that… Get started!

You might be wondering at this point why there has to be so many steps before "Go!" Well, because there'll always be an excitement stage, which is quickly replaced by a reality stage. And the truth about the reality stage is that it really isn't fun.

It's like going to a college basketball game and wanting to be on the team before considering the thousands of hours spent practicing without cameras, in empty gyms, with no fanfare. Take action behind the scenes right away, while you give the excitement phase time to cool down before you jump out there for everyone to see. Otherwise, you'll start and not be able to finish.

After you've done your To Do List, go ahead and do what you're scared of! Remember, fear isn't a bad thing. Most of the major things we do in our lives bring us through different stages of fear. It's giving in to it that's not ok!

Action item: Need to build up your fear resume a little? One thing you can do is talk to strangers. It's the easiest way to do something you're scared of without endangering yourself.

When we were younger, our parents told us not to talk to strangers. Although it was wise advice then, for many of us talking to strangers is still stuck in our heads as something scary. So the first thing I want you to do is go somewhere and talk to someone you don't know (if you're in college or younger, make sure you talk to someone in your peer group).

Talking to a stranger (in a public place like Applebee's or Starbucks) won't kill you. I promise! Actually, I've met some of the most interesting people by starting random conversations at restaurants or airports. One time, I even met a bounty hunter, just like the ones in the movies!

The best thing is, that even if you say the dumbest, most embarrassing thing ever in life, you'll probably never see that person again.

It's like gambling with Monopoly money. What do you really have to lose?

When you start doing things you're scared of, you'll stop looking at people who do those same things as super-human, because you'll be one of them. The quicker you beat Fear, the quicker you start building confidence!

Step 2
LOOK, FEEL, PLAY

"Being pretty is fun."

People are always saying, "It's what's on the inside that counts." And they aren't completely lying. I mean, I'll take a good heart over a pretty face any day. But let's not pretend that how we feel has nothing to do with how we look, or that people always treat everyone equally, regardless of appearance.

Not even the nicest person can say they do that. Plus as women we all have an inherent need to feel pretty, and to any fellas reading this, y'all know you want to look good too!

One of the things we say all the time in the sports world is, **"Look good, feel good. Feel good, play good."** It works in life too! Don't get me wrong; YOU'RE ALREADY PRETTY, but it's important to do everything you can to be the best looking version of you possible.

Notice I said, of YOU. This chapter isn't about trying to CHANGE your look. Instead, we're going to talk about different ways to IMPROVE it.

I realize this can be a touchy subject because we don't want to act like worth and confidence only come from how we look. But doing things to look better doesn't make us superficial any more than taking a shower or wearing deodorant does. Getting better has to improve every part of us, including how we look. Why would we ignore the first thing everyone else sees?

The difference between bettering yourself and changing yourself means everything. It's not like you have to completely makeover your look in order to feel more confident. Sometimes all it takes is something small and it'll make you feel like a brand new person!

For me, I'll look in the mirror ask myself, what do I feel most self-conscious about that's within my power to change? Whether that means getting my hair done, or working out a little more, or buying a hot color of lipstick, I'll do it.

So for you, what is that? Is there anything that bugs you every time you walk out the door about how you look? And I'm not talking about anything you'd have to hire a surgeon to fix – we'll touch on that in a second. I'm talking about surface changes you can make that will put that little pep in your step.

Remember the last time you got a hair cut you loved or put on that new outfit? You felt fab right? Make sure you're keeping up with those things and you'll feel like you deserve to think more of yourself!

***

Where we get in trouble is when we define "pretty" or "looking good" as one thing and one thing only.

In the conversation about feeling pretty, we have to identify exactly what "pretty" means. How pretty you feel has a lot to do with who and what you see as pretty. So we ALL need to define it for ourselves... and picking a beauty role model can help us do that.

Beauty role model: Someone who makes you feel great about how you look because of how she looks.

When I was in high school, I wanted to look like all the popular girls. Unfortunately most of them were petite, preppy, "cheerleader types" and I was 6'6", completely a tomboy and played basketball.

That didn't exactly help me feel super confident about my appearance. Actually, I hated how I looked for most of high school and always wished that somehow I could look like them...

Until I met Lisa Leslie. She was 6'5", athletic, played basketball and modeled on the side. Oh, and absolutely beautiful! Lisa helped me redefine my standard of beauty and showed me that I didn't have to look like the other girls to be pretty.

She was someone I could realistically look like one day! And that's what a beauty role model should be: inspiration to look as good as you can without trying to look completely different.

The process of choosing your beauty role model is important. If you're built thin, like I am, then stop looking at all of these curvy, video girls as your definition of pretty. Of course that's going to make you feel too skinny and have you trying to get fake boobs and butt implants!

Instead, look at someone like Zoe Saldana. Did you see her in the movie Columbiana? She's amazing and also super skinny. So if you're built more like her, look at her and girls like her as your example of pretty!

If you are a thick girl, get Zoe Saldana out of your head! You're never going to look like that so of course she's going to make you feel fat and have you trying to starve yourself.

Instead, look at someone like Candice Huffine. She's a fabulous, plus-sized model that's always representing beautiful for curvy girls everywhere. She'll make you excited and proud to embrace your body shape.

The key to picking a beauty role model is to pick someone who makes you feel better about the way you look because of the way she looks. It should be someone with similar characteristics as you who's working them to the fullest.

One of my beauty role models now is Gabrielle Union. I picked her because she's brown-skinned, has black girl hair but always rockin' a great weave, built thin but athletic, and beautiful with a big smile. She's someone fabulous who makes me feel better about how I look because of how she looks!

Also, when I cut my hair and went natural a few years back, I had to adjust my image of beauty to help me with the transition. So I "unfollowed" every girl on Instagram that was going to make me wish I had my long, straight weave back, and followed a bunch of natural girls instead.

You can take a lot control over how you feel about beauty simply by editing what you see and hear every day!

No matter what you look like, there's people out there who look similar and have made it work for them. You just have to find them. I know you can!

***

The fight to feel pretty doesn't end with convincing ourselves that we are. Unfortunately, we all have the potential to be influenced by the opinions and definitions of those around us.

I was talking to this guy a while back and one day he told me, "I don't date dark girls." I was like, "Umm, have you seen me? I'm definitely brown!" To which he said, "You're light enough."

I wish I could say that his thought process was unique and just because he was a jerk, but that wasn't the only time I've had someone assure me that I shouldn't worry because I'm "light enough" to be "pretty." The worst part is that each time, it was meant as a compliment!

Please understand that even though this example mentions skin color, it's really not about skin color!

This is about the fight we're ALL involved in, between what they tell us is true about ourselves and what we need to believe in order to love ourselves!

Whether it's color or body type or hair or cup size, we still have to live in this body, with all the characteristics we can't change, no matter what anyone thinks about it. It forces us to ask the question: Are we only as pretty as they say we are?

The truth is, I don't think I'm prettier when I'm lighter. I love coming home in the summer and finding well placed tan lines. But no matter what I - or you - think, this world will still try to convince us that we are indeed, only as pretty or acceptable as other people see us.

It's our responsibility to OURSELVES not to buy in.

Yes, I can sit here and wonder how dark my skin will get in the summer – or if I'm skinny enough to wear a bikini…or if my hair is too frizzy…or any of the other questions we all ask to torture ourselves. It's what we've been conditioned to do and we can't stop those thoughts from coming. What we can control though, is how those thoughts impact our lives.

Will we stay inside or cover up even when we don't want to? Will we change things we love about ourselves just to be more acceptable to others? Will we obsess over what "they" think?

These things we CAN choose.

And I choose NO. I had to make the choice not to let fears of incompetence and anyone else's definition of pretty in shape, color, beauty or other stop me from experiencing. And I won't believe anyone who tells me I'm less than because of something I can't change.

But I can't make that decision for you; only you can. So what do you think? Are you ready to try your hardest to jump over the fear of what others think about your version of pretty in order to build your own confidence? (I hope you're yelling, "YES!" right now).

Taking some time to pick your beauty role model will definitely help, so go for it!

***

Let's look at this discussion of beauty from a little different angle.

Question: Who's prettier? Beyoncé or Katy Perry?

Depending on who you ask, you'll get different answers. So does that mean Katy should feel ugly just because some people would say Beyoncé is prettier? Of course not.

I had a teammate who used to say, "I may not be a 10, but I clean up well." I love that phrase! Not everyone will rate us a "10" on their personal "pretty scale." We can't change that. What other people think about our bodies and us is their business. All we can do is be the prettiest version of ourselves, and then work to be confident in that.

Beyoncé will never look like Katy. Katy will never look like Beyoncé. And neither of us is going to look like either of them. Let people rate you as they choose. Your job is to clean up well.

The next step to being confident in how you look is to get some evidence.

We all have those times when we stand in front of the mirror and pick out everything that's wrong with us. For me it usually happens when I watch something like the Victoria Secret Fashion Show and forget everything we just talked about. Been there, done that.

When you're having one of those moments, walk away from the mirror.

Besides walking away from the mirror, something else that helps me feel better about how I look, in those times especially, are what I call "evidence pictures."

So often we're tempted to believe that us feeling some way means things are that way.

But question. Have you ever felt like something was true, I mean really felt it down to the bottom of your soul, and then found out it wasn't? I have a few relationships in that category (laughing).

The fact that it's happened to all of us is proof that our feelings lie, no matter how true they feel sometimes. And the best way to call out a lie is to confront it with evidence.

So an "evidence picture" is any picture that you think you look good in. Like you took it and were like, "Ok me, I see you!" (laughing). That way, whenever you feel unpretty, you can pull out that picture as evidence that the way you feel at that given moment isn't a fact.

I personally do this all the time. When I don't feel pretty I'll go to my Instagram page and find the last day I looked pretty. It's my way of showing myself, "See, you couldn't have turned ugly in 3 days!"

So go find you some evidence pictures and don't be afraid to use them!

Another way you can use the concept of evidence pictures for confidence in things other than looks is to create what some people call a "praise file." Awards, accomplishments, emails, texts, cards, compliments and any other self-affirming things you can find. When you feel dumb, insignificant, bad at everything, unloved or any of the other negative things we tell ourselves about ourselves, use them as proof that you're wrong.

It's similar to your fear resume in that it can help you fight back against the negative things we hear, from ourselves or anybody else. Later in this book we'll go into detail about some ways we can lessen or eliminate those voices but first, we have to learn how to fight them off.

***

The great thing is that as you start improving how you look, you can use your outer change to inspire inner growth.

One way outward changes in our looks can become inward confidence in our self is to confront the insecurities that we have about our looks, head on.

I was at the beauty salon a few years ago and my hairdresser told me I needed to cut my hair short and wear it without a weave because it was damaged. Right away I thought, "Oh my gosh I can't cut my hair! Then I won't be pretty!" That thought caught me totally off guard and I had to check myself like, "Hold on…so the only thing that makes you pretty is this long, fake hair?"

Right then, because of a belief I didn't even know I had before, I told her, "Cut it off."

I needed to take off the false security blanket of long hair to prove to myself that I could feel pretty without it. Remember, Visible Confidence doesn't come off with anything you can take off. I had to build that. I'll be honest with you in that the look was completely different and some days I didn't feel as pretty. But most days I did. The best thing about it was that in addition to pretty, I felt powerful!

There is power in confronting the insecurities we have about ourselves and flipping them upside down.

Once I knew I could feel pretty without the fake hair, wearing it was no longer a need, but an option. In every area of life there is power in having choices! With power comes confidence.

So I'll ask you, what security blankets do you have? Is there anything you think, "Wow, I could never feel good about myself without this"? Maybe it's your hair or skimpy clothes like it was for me. Or maybe it's your designer purses, your car, who your friends are or your high-powered career.

I'm not telling you to be extreme and cut your hair, sell your car, dump your friends and quit your job (laughing). Simply realizing insecurities in the foundation of who you are and then taking small steps to correct them can translate into confidence well beyond just how you look.

Answer these questions:
Where does my pretty come from?
Is there anything I wasn't born with that I couldn't be confident without?
How can I lessen the hold that thing has on my self-image?

A few ideas:
If it's your designer clothes, try going somewhere with no-name stuff on. Don't look like a bum but wear the simplest, most average thing you own, no purse and no name brand shoes. Do you feel any different? Practice acting confident without all those things to help you.

If it's your career that gives you that extra validation, try to keep from mentioning it to people unless it's necessary. I actually had to do this. The company I used to work for was well known in the industry and I noticed that I was starting to place too much emphasis on that when people asked me what I did. I had been subtly bragging without even meaning to.

So I stopped telling people the company name unless they specifically asked. Same with the school I went to or the teams I played for. I never want to feel like my worth is coming from those things so I don't use them unless it's practical.

What's crazy though is that when you learn to shine on your own, without using your resume or what you own, people will want to know more about you. They'll stay in contact or look you up. When they find out what you could've bragged about but chose not to, they'll respect you even more for it.

But in order to do that, you have to feel like enough on your own, whether or not they know "what your body looks like", "who you are," "what you have," or "what you do."

What about relationships with high-powered people? It's not like you have to dump all of your friends, but if your validation comes from that, I'd encourage you to start placing a higher value on people's character instead of their titles. This was another thing I had to do just because of the industry I was in.

All this may sound a little bit extreme, but it's all about building complete confidence in you and only you.

You will never learn to be confident in you while being completely sustained by everything else.

Making sure your pretty comes from the right places is key to building Visible Confidence.

PRACTICAL: *Find your beauty role model and then be more like her.*

Pick someone who makes you feel great about the way you already look. DO NOT pick someone who looks any way that you never could. Be realistic with yourself. Once you have your beauty role model, what can you do to highlight the positives about your look like she does? Work on doing that.

If one of your goals is to lose weight, make sure you pick someone that may be in better shape than you at the moment, but still has a similar body type. Your beauty role model should inspire you to be better without making you feel ugly along the way. Improve what you can control.

Also, what role does TV and social media play in your image of beauty? Stop watching and "unfollow" anything and anyone that makes you feel worse about how you look. Mold your own image of beauty and take back the control of your confidence!

Step 3
SHINE FROM THE INSIDE

"Vanity is good when it keeps you looking good.
Vanity is bad when looking good is all that matters."

I have a confession to make: I am 100% for plastic surgery. If I ever need work done to feel like I still look good as I get older, you better believe I'll get it. And yes, MAC make-up, Nordstrom's and Brazilian wavy hair make me feel as fabulous as the next girl.

I think that in general, if any of that is going to help you feel better about yourself, do it.

For example, people always ask me if I whitened my teeth. And the answer is always yes. My teeth were straight but weren't white, so I got them bleached, once in college and again a couple years ago. It was totally worth it.

BUT - and I can't emphasize this enough - if you think those things alone are going to solve all of your confidence issues or make you automatically feel "good enough," you're wrong.

You see, I've been there – all made up, wearing designer clothes and a killer weave, hating on the girl across the room because I thought she was still prettier. Or getting hit on all the time, but as soon as one guy doesn't call my thoughts automatically jump to the conclusion that it's because I'm not pretty enough.

I'm not the only one though. Look at the starlets we idolize but who frequently admit to having self-esteem issues, eating disorders and drug problems. And let us tell it, they always LOOK perfect!

How is that even possible?

It's because anything we do ON the outside only gives us confidence IN the outside.

It makes it easier to step out and feel like you look good. It's easier to talk to someone when you feel pretty. People treat you a certain way because of how you look, and it's fun. But is that what makes you, *you?* If your identity comes from your looks and how others respond to those looks, then your confidence will always be at their mercy. Like we talked about with Beyoncé and Katy, no matter how pretty you are, there will always be someone out there who thinks another girl is prettier. And when you run into that person, your confidence will be shot. You are handing them the ability to crush you.

It's not just you. I've done it before too.

When I graduated from college I knew that playing in the WNBA was going to be amazing. I was coming from Vanderbilt as a 2-time All-American and the school's All-Time Leading Scorer. Sacramento had picked me 2nd overall in the draft, which would usually mean they had high hopes for me. Unfortunately it wasn't what I expected when I got there.

One time in particular, I was in the weight room with our trainer about to lift after practice. As I stepped on the scale to weigh in, my coach walked up, looked at the number and immediately told me I needed to lose 20 pounds if I ever wanted to be good enough to play.

I was shocked. 20 pounds is a lot to lose when you're at the weight you've always played at and weren't planning on losing any! The worst thing was that our trainer, a woman, agreed with him.

I had no idea what to say. I wish I had told him exactly what I thought of him and then worked that much harder to prove him wrong. But I didn't. Instead of having confidence in being the type of player that had made me successful, I took his opinion for fact and made up my mind to lose the weight, no questions asked.

When that WNBA season ended, I went overseas to play and went on what I called my "yogurt and tuna fish diet," while going through two practices a day. It bordered on starvation.

Some days I was so tired I could barely run up and down the court. Other times I had to take a bathroom break to sit down because I was so dizzy. But I was willing to do anything to be my coach's definition of good enough.

And even though my overseas season was terrible, I came back 20 pounds lighter to a coach who raved about how hard I had obviously worked in the off-season. Right before he traded me to another team two weeks later.

That's the thing: Sometimes, you can give people exactly what they want from you and your best still won't be good enough for them.

That's why it's so important that we don't focus on just the outside, or change who we are for other people. It's crazy because there are countless times like that where I had every reason to be confident, yet was still stumbling around, worrying about what others thought of me and trying to make myself good enough to feel good enough. I didn't feel really confident until I was able to say, "Forget it. This is me and if you don't like it then someone else will," *and mean it.*

So the question is, "How do you get to the point where you can say that and not be lying?"

The answer? Put in as much work on the inside as you do on the outside.

The coach of my new team appreciated my game for what it had been. After that season he asked me to gain back the weight I'd lost so I could be the player I was meant to be. It felt so good to hear someone not only say what I needed to hear, but believe it was true.

I didn't just start eating more. I got in the weight room for real. I worked out four hours a day, six days a week with a personal trainer doing basketball workouts, dynamic strength exercises and nutrition improvement. The numbers on the scale and how I looked didn't matter. Instead, I did what I should've done from the beginning: be me and get better from the ground up, instead of just catering to someone else's opinion.

You will never find you until you stop trying to please them.

This improvement project wasn't only on the basketball side of things. I started working on me as a person too. I stopped dating random people and drinking every time I went out. I got back to reading books and writing, which was something I loved but hadn't done much since college. It was during that time that I also discovered my love for helping people make sense of this crazy world we're all trying to figure out, which gave me a sense of purpose.

I did it all so that the next time someone told me to change myself to fit his picture of what I should be, I could say, "No," without being affected. And so that the next time I needed encouragement to get back to being me, I could tell myself, instead of hoping my coach or anyone else would say it for me. I got better so that the next time, me being "good enough" could come from the inside and not the outside.

Be enough for you even when it's not enough for them!

This mindset and the process it inspires don't just apply to me. It applies to all of us! Just like outer confidence comes from doing things to look better, inner confidence comes from doing things to BE better. Don't change the outside without looking at the inside that made the change necessary in the first place.

That'd be like spray-painting your grass green without fixing the fact that you're growing brown grass.

When you get better on the inside, you'll see the change. You'll be able to smile at that girl across the room and tell her she's beautiful, even if you think she's prettier than you. She won't automatically be a threat because you'll know there's more to you than just what you look like.

When that guy or girl doesn't call, you'll know they're missing out instead of feeling like you are. Because you'll be confident in everything else you have to offer someone, in addition to your looks.

And when people tell you to change who you are to be good enough, you'll be able to tell them "no." Because you worked hard to become the person you are and you refuse to let her go that easily.

There's nothing wrong with doing everything you can to look better, as long as it's not only on the outside. In order for confidence to go beyond shallow and fake, working on the inside isn't an option. *It's a requirement.*

***

As we continue to get better, one of the most important ingredients in our lives is consciousness. That's not exactly a word most of us think about every day. Let's talk about it.

Have you ever been walking through the mall not realizing what song is playing until you find yourself humming it afterwards? Then you're like, "Oh yeah, that was playing earlier!" It's different than when you're in the car singing at the top of your lungs to your favorite song, right?

Well, that's kind of how consciousness applies to life.

A lot of times we get so caught up in the emotion and grind of everyday life that we forget to step back and take a look at exactly what we're doing. Then we get to a point where we look up like, "Wait...How the heck did I get here?"

Like when you realize your best friend isn't really your best friend anymore, you're way outta shape, or that your significant other has been stressing you out for way too long. You wonder how you let it get so far away from right. I've definitely been there.

But what if we were paying attention as we went along, to prevent that "how did I get here" moment? That's what consciousness is. It's living in each moment, appreciating it for what's happening. It's also paying attention to where you're going so that you're not surprised when you get there.

So every now and then, we need to intentionally pause and step outside of life's hurricane to take an honest, rational (translated: unemotional) look at it before jumping back in.

This actually happens a lot right around the New Year. People take an inventory of their life and figure out what they need to do to get better. That's why we all get so excited about getting a new start around the New Year. But living a conscious life means taking that inventory way more than once a year, so that you can turn around before you get too far down the wrong path.

Make this a habit. Maybe you do it once a week or once a month, where you intentionally look around at what's going on to make sure you're still going where you want to be going.

Because there's no autopilot on a successful life for any of us. No, hold the steering wheel, pay attention and turn when necessary.

Be conscious in your actions and thoughts, and the direction they're taking you. When we look around and intentionally observe the journey, we'll be able to keep moving forward on the road we want to be on.

Don't just hear. Sing!

***

In addition to confidence, the best thing that comes as a result of working on you from the inside is authenticity.

Authenticity is when what you say = what you do = who you are.

I got one of the best compliments the other day from someone I used to play basketball against. She said, "You know, I've always appreciated the fact that you were you, even when you didn't completely know who that was."

The thing about authenticity is that you don't have to tell people everything. But what you do tell them, in word and action, has to be true.

Authenticity just might be the most magnetic of all qualities, after confidence, because it draws people to you, even when they're not exactly sure why they're coming. It's because we were all created with the desire to be true to ourselves, and so we recognize that when we see it in others.

The biggest barrier to authenticity is our doubt that people will like the real us if we show it to them. But one of my favorite quotes from the Velveteen Rabbit promises that, "once you are Real, you can't be ugly, except to those who don't understand."

This is so true. I've never known a person – I mean really known someone –who I saw as authentic and unattractive at the same time. That's why people who fully embrace themselves don't have to be "classically pretty" to be beautiful.

The problem we face is that the moment we don't believe Real is beautiful, there are so many influencers ready and waiting to tell us what else we should be. So we neglect our own voices because the others are louder, and sometimes more persuasive!

It can be easy to assume someone else knows better, especially when it feels like you don't know much at all. The truth is, they might know how to be them better than you know how to be you. That's what makes them Real. But you trying to be them will make you fake.

I used to deal with this a lot. When I was younger, I always wanted to be that super-hot, in your face, sexy girl. Like Adrianna Lima. But that so wasn't me (laughing). Whenever I tried to be that girl, I felt fake and failed miserably. I am much more the down-to-earth, chill, playfully pretty in my own way girl. That's another reason Gabrielle Union is my beauty role model, because she comes off as kind of like that too.

One of the hardest things is finding and then accepting who you are when it's not who you want to be. But keep in mind there are amazing women in every type. The real you is more magnetic than the fake you will ever be, no matter how awesome people think the fake you is.

You'll never be authentic until you get to know the person you are more than the person you're being.

Find you instead. Experiment, make mistakes, laugh, cry and experience. Find your own voice, own character, own person, and be that. I wish I had a short recipe on how to do all that, but there really isn't one.

One tip I can give you is to pay attention along the way so that you don't keep trying stuff that clearly isn't helping. The goal is to laugh more than you cry, and to make mistakes but not repeat them.

As you try different things, if it fits you, do it until it doesn't. If – or when – you reach a point where it doesn't fit, stop and try something else. Sometimes you'll find the real "you" underneath hurt, adversity and other people's expectations.

Sometimes "you" needs to be built up or put back together. But even then, it's ok to show that to others as long as you keep fighting. Fighters inspire. It's through the journey that you'll discover what "real" looks like for you. And Real passes Pretty on the way to Beautiful every time.

For all of us, "real" is made up of our strengths, weaknesses, deepest needs, desires, and dreams. One thing on that list scares most of us: our weaknesses. In dealing with them, we'll go to one extreme or another: we either try our hardest to ignore them and act like they don't exist, or we focus on them so much that they distract us from what we're actually good at.

The thing is, we can't be authentic without acknowledging our weaknesses and we'll never be productive if they're all we focus on!

To fix this, we turn to Kanye. Near the beginning of his career, he said one of the simplest, most profound things:

He said, "Everything I'm not made me everything I am."

That statement is so true. Know your weaknesses. Acknowledge them so they don't sabotage your life. But don't treat them like they're the end all, be all of who you are. You also have strengths that complement those weaknesses. If you learn to use your strengths correctly, they'll make your weaknesses irrelevant, for all practical things anyway.

When I went to the Gallup Strengths Academy, they referred to this concept as "balconies and basements." We all have balconies and basements in our personalities, meaning strengths and weaknesses we're naturally born with. If you had a balcony to decorate, why would you ever insist on hanging out in the basement all the time?

Live in your strengths because you don't have time to get great at everything. Stick to what you're good at and get great at it!

A lot of people are going to tell you to take your weaknesses and make them strengths. And I'm going to tell you that's completely wrong. Instead, separate your weaknesses into two categories: those you need to compensate for and those you need to improve on.

Weaknesses that we need to compensate for are things that we're weak at but that aren't necessarily getting any better. I'll use myself as an example. I am super absent minded. I always have a zillion things going on in my head and they get thought and then they get forgotten. So I've have to build things into my life to make sure I can compensate for that.

For example, when I park in a parking garage, I take a picture of where I parked, because there's no chance I'm going to remember when I come out.

If I have to call someone at 2 p.m., I set an alarm. Because it'll be 3pm and I'll be like, "Didn't I have something to do?"

Those are things I've done to compensate for my absent mindedness. What I'm not going to do is take a bunch of memory classes or beat myself up for forgetting stuff. It's something I'm weak at that's probably not going to get any better! So what are some weaknesses that you can put in that category and help yourself out?

The other bucket of weaknesses is the ones we need to improve on. These are things that you're not naturally good at but there's no way you'll ever be successful if you don't improve on them.

For example, I'm not a naturally disciplined person. Most people think I am but I'm really not at all. I compensate for this a little bit by surrounding myself with people who can hold me accountable to my goals. But at the same time, I need to improve on that. So I've started to write things down because I get excited when I can check them off, I put up my goals in my room so they remind me what I'm chasing every day, holding me accountable whenever I look at them.

Another way you can get better at things you're weak at is to use something you're good at instead. For example, I'm really competitive. So while I might not do something because I'm disciplined and need to get it done, I'll definitely do it if I'm competing with someone else. So I need to surround myself with people I can compete with.

A great example of this is the gym. I wasn't working out and so I went and got a gym membership to help me. The first one I got was at this gym where people who don't want to feel embarrassed standing next to some fitness model go to workout. But when I went there, relative to everyone else, I was still in pretty good shape. So I didn't feel the need to compete and I didn't have enough discipline to keep going.

Then I changed gyms to one where a lot of athletes and former athletes work out. It reminded me what kind of shape I use to be in every time I looked at them. So I was not only trying to get on their level but I was also competing with me 5 years ago. The element of competition keeps me going even when my discipline won't.

I'm not saying make your weaknesses your strengths. I'll never be the most disciplined person in the world. But there are ways to improve on them or to get the same results.

Why does this relate to confidence and authenticity? Because if we can admit our weaknesses instead of being so embarrassed that we hide them, it makes us more authentic to other people. And it's a lot easier to admit things that aren't ruining your life or making you less successful.

***

We talked about finding a beauty role model in the last chapter. But should getting better on the inside affect who your beauty role model is?

The discussion on character just might make you choose a different beauty role model. Or maybe you need two: one for appearance and one for character. There's nothing wrong with that. It's like going one place for your eye-brow threading and another for your manicure. Whatever gets the job done, right?

So the question here is, who do you want to inspire the way you live your life?

If we aim to be beautiful on both the inside and the outside, we need to choose people who are living that out. In general, too many of us celebrate women who look beautiful and act ugly. Or in the case of men, it's usually the ones who are successful but ugly in their actions. And that leads us to either become who we look up to, or think less of who we are because it doesn't look like them.

Please understand, those people go home and have to take off everything they put on.

None of the makeup, clothes, shoes, bags or titles are part of them. Whatever is on the inside that shows through in their actions doesn't come off.

I know that because I used to be on the inside of that circle. I used to be that girl. And I've had people want to be like me, when I didn't even want to be like me, but used everything I could get my hands on to pretend I did.

I did it so they would continue wanting to be like me and maybe one day I would too. I filled my life with so many other things so I couldn't hear my own heart, mind, past and hurts.

When people's actions are ugly, cheap, messy, or overly flashy, there's a good chance their peace is low and their true confidence in who they are is even lower. No one is born acting that way. They're acting ugly because they're actually broken.

And you need to know that. Because too many people are looking at others, beating themselves up like, "Oh my gosh why are they so confident and happy and I'm not?" But that person's actions are showing you that behind closed doors she really isn't either.

I'm definitely not saying you can't wear nice things or be successful and still be confident in yourself. That was the whole point of chapter two. But if your actions don't match your appearance then something is missing.

Real confidence doesn't demand attention, put other people down of brag about all the reasons for that confidence. So this affects your beauty role model because it won't make you more confident to imitate someone who isn't really confident.

Once I started to really believe in myself, it was a lot easier to stay that way when I stopped comparing myself to the outward appearance of someone whose actions showed she was a mess on the inside. Stop judging your entire self based on your limited and skewed view of that person. It's not fair to you and it's even less productive.

So who are these people? Well, depends on your definition of character and the type of life you want to live. I stopped watching Scandal because it's about a beautiful, smart, talented woman who makes herself ugly (character wise) by being a sidepiece to a married man.

If I one day aspire to be a wife (which I do), I don't need to fill my head with glamorous images of a type of relationship that I want no part of. This goes for men too. There are countless examples of men on TV in less than honest relationships with women.

Full transparency here, I've been the other woman – not to someone who was married but to someone who was dating. And at that point, I wasn't confident and my character wasn't where it needed to be. If you're there too, I understand but stop and make the decision to work on both.

Some people say it's just TV or just a show. But let's be honest with ourselves. It's hard to watch some of those shows and not want to be like those people or at least have their lifestyle, even if it's only a little. The things we feed our minds plant desires in our hearts. So no, it's not just TV. Or just music. Or movies.

I'm sharing my personal opinions here. You get to pick your own criteria for your beauty role model and who you want to be like.

We become who we admire. Yes, those women seem confident but if you're going to start choosing new people to look up to, pick someone who is the total package with visible confidence in who she is, and the character to support it.

Or, as I said before, don't hesitate to pick two, or several like I have. Highlight the good things in different people and use those as motivation to be the best version of yourself. This is not about judging!

It's to make sure you don't get caught up trying to imitate the total package of someone who isn't really the total package.

So you see, while the outside will always be what people notice first and can give us a confidence boost, it really is what's on the inside that counts as far as Visible Confidence goes. Let's make sure that while doing everything to improve how we look, we're also taking intentional, practical steps to improve who we are.

PRACTICAL: Go stand in front of the mirror. If it showed your character instead of your appearance, would you like what you saw?

If the answer is yes, then keep doing what you're doing, but remember that even "nice" people have things they need to work on. Maybe it's something outside of yourself, like reaching out to help people. Don't settle. In fact, the more you can improve, the more confident you'll be. So be picky if you have to for the sake of being better.

If the answer is no, be honest with yourself about why. Then work on changing it. It won't be easy and you'll probably have to do some things you don't like (more on that later). But the reward is that you'll automatically feel more confident in being the total package.

Then, do something to invest in yourself. Read a book about a subject you can discuss at work or around your friends. Find a hobby that you can be good at. Start a journal. Work out. Learn how to cook something new. Do anything you can to be more well rounded. Because the more you have to offer the world, the more confident you'll be in it.

Step 4
WORK

"Come to work to work."

My college basketball coaches taught me how to be an All-American in three days. After my first practice freshman year, my head coach, Coach Foster, walked me over to my position coach, Coach Gaudet, and said, "You guys are going to work out together for a little while." I looked at him like he was crazy. I mean, I had just experienced one of the hardest practices of my life and now he wanted me to do more? But since I couldn't exactly tell coach no, we stayed out there for another 30 minutes.

The next day, after practice, Coach Foster walked me down to Coach Gaudet and said, "You guys are going to work out together for a little while." And we spent another 30 minutes. The third day of practice, he did the same.

The next day, after practice I saw Coach Gaudet start to leave and go back to his office. I ran over to him and was like, "Hey! Aren't we going to work out?" He smiled and replied in his classic, sarcastic humor, "Well why didn't you say so sooner?"

I saw Coach Foster smile as he watched us get started. And for as long as they were my coaches, we worked extra every day after practice. Sometimes it was a hard 30 minutes and others it was a quick five-minute drill or a film session in his office. But no matter what we did, it was consistent, focused work.

Legendary basketball coach, Pat Summitt, said that, **"Confidence is what happens when you've done the work that entitles you to succeed."**

Such a profound and true statement. My coaches taught me that in three days and it was reinforced over the rest of my college career. Whether it's on the inside or the outside, one thing that never changes in the confidence process is WORK.

When you're working towards confidence in something, you have to be willing to do two things:

Be bad at it for a little while so that you can get good at it.

So often we want to be perfect at something right away and so when we're not, we stop doing it. But if you ever want to get good at something, you have to be willing to work through being bad at it. And usually we're our worst critics. You're probably not as bad at is as you think you are. Give yourself a ton of grace.

Hate being bad enough to make that "getting good" happen as quickly as possible.

Some people are satisfied being mediocre or average at things. And so they only put in enough work to get to that level. But we're not stupid and we can't fool ourselves. Average skills will never produce over the top confidence, no matter how much positive self-talk you do or nice clothes you wear. So it's super important to refuse to settle for being average and make that good to great happen as quickly as possible.

The thing about confidence is that you don't get to a point and automatically you're confident. With every mistake you make and fix, you're earning your confidence, little by little. It's the process of proving yourself to you.

Once you prove it to yourself, it's ok to believe it.

The other thing about work is that is needs to be focused. And this is a huge one because if you're like me – and I think you are in this way – the willingness to work isn't the biggest problem. Instead it's usually a question of, "What do I work at? Where do I focus my energy?"

We want to say yes to everything and a lot of us are talented enough to succeed at a few different things. We have so many ideas and things we want to do and chances to do this and this and this that we're not quite sure what to say yes to.

I was talking to a friend about this the other day. She was telling me how her hearts desire and calling was to be a nurse. And we graduated around the same time so she had been out of school for a while and was looking at going back for nursing.

The school she graduated from was offering her a full scholarship to get her masters in psychology, but she couldn't use the money for nursing because they didn't have a nursing program. So she had a huge decision to make. The scholarship was a "great opportunity." And no one likes to turn down free money, right? But in two years when she finished her psychology degree, she wouldn't be any closer to what she really wanted to do, which was nursing. So I asked her one question: Do you really want to be a nurse?

Because the bottom line is this: going to school for psychology and putting in all the work to get a degree in two years would get her no closer to her ultimate goal of being a nurse.

It doesn't matter how great an opportunity is, if it's not taking you in the direction you want to go, it's not a great opportunity for you at that moment.

I think a lot of us do the same thing. We're working so hard, but all the energy we're expending isn't focused in one direction. It's shooting all over the place. It's like running in a circle but going nowhere. Then we wonder why we're tired.

This was something I really struggled with last year. I was saying yes to almost everything. It got to the point where I was working a full time job, throwing brunch parties for charity, organizing and hosting conversation events, leading a ministry at church, volunteering at an after school program, going to a bunch of social events and trying to write this book.

At the end of the day I was mentally and physically exhausted from being busy, and also discouraged because I knew I hadn't made time for one of the biggest things that was going to move me forward.

Everything I was doing was positive, but it wasn't all helping me get to my ultimate goal of building a self-sustaining business. My problem wasn't a lack of work. It was a lack of focus.

So I put my foot down and decided I couldn't keep doing all that. When you get to this point you have to train yourself to do two things:

Stop. Just stop. Before you say yes to that newest request, or take off sprinting after that new, brilliant idea you just had, stop.

And then after you stop, ask yourself: Is this action getting me closer to what I want?

If I can't say YES in all caps with three exclamation points after, I say no. It's really that simple. No more doing things just because it's a good thing to do. If we're going to work towards purpose, our steps have to be purposeful.

Now of course, sometimes you might have to do something that's a means to an end. And that's ok. But it's important to be clear about what the end destination is. That way every action is taking you closer to that point.

This has made so much of a difference in my life! I'm not running around like a crazy person, getting mad at people who need some of my time because I don't have any to spare, and most importantly, I have time for the things I've prioritized as most important.

Clarifying what you're working for is just as important as deciding to work for it.

So I'm asking you the same question I asked my friend: What do you really want? What are you working towards in life and in business? What is the confidence you're building in this book going to help you get?

Take some time to get clear about everything you're working towards.

Once we decide what we want, the hard part for all of us is having the discipline to line up our daily actions with that list because it means we have to say a lot of "no's" to things that aren't necessarily bad but aren't high enough on the priority list to justify the time it would take away from those other things.

So with that in mind, here are three steps that can help you do that.

DO put things in a working order.

This is so important. There has to be an unquestioned priority #1. And it isn't necessarily the thing you like the most, or the one that's most valuable.

Number one should be the one thing that makes everything else in your life possible and going the way it should.

For example, before I became a full time entrepreneur, I had to prioritize my job first, even though I wanted to spend more time in my business because my business wasn't self-sustaining yet. Now I'm in a season where my first priority as far as work goes is my business, but it took a while to get there.

So for you, what's the thing that will cause everything else to fall if it does? That's your number one. Once you have that, number down from there.

DON'T do #2 at the expense of #1.

You can have different interests and be doing different things. I know I usually am. But when it's time to work, you have to be able to get it done. If you don't take care of #1, everything falls apart and you can't do any of it. So if those different responsibilities start getting in the way of your first priority, you need to start taking things off your list until you can do it all.

This is important for those times when things conflict. Of course you're going to try to do #1 and #2 and maybe #3 and #4. But what happens when something is going on at the same time or they conflict in another way? Which one do you choose?

That's why this list is so important. The order of your priorities has to be absolutely clear, not only on paper, but also in action.

DO go hard.

People love the saying, "work hard, play hard," for a reason. No matter what you're doing, work or play, do it 100%. A lot of times we get so caught up in working that we don't make time to do the things we work so hard for.

And how many times does that leave us feeling burnt out and bitter? Treat yourself! Playing hard will make the hard work worth it and remind you what you're working so hard for!

Work for your reward. Reward yourself for your work. And then, do it all over again.

Clarifying your priorities will literally change your life! Be intentional about doing it and sticking to it.

***

I can promise that if you're working enough to earn the type of confidence you want, at some point you're going to want to quit. No matter how much you want what you're working for or love what you're doing, no one enjoys making mistakes. No one loves failure. There will be that time – or a few – when you'll want to say, "Forget it," and do something easier.

But that's awesome! Because every time we want to quit and decide not to, we build more confidence in ourselves and our ability to do hard things. I've definitely been through the "I want to quit" cycle a few times. One of the best examples is when I left my job in coaching for one in medical device sales.

I had spent my entire adult life working in the sports industry. So when I made the jump to med sales, I had a ton of catching up to do. I'd work a full day, going in and out of hospitals trying to make contacts, and then come home and study for hours at night, trying to learn everything about this field I knew nothing about. I felt like my brain was on information overload!

I was intent on making it work but I was also overwhelmed, completely exhausted, and to top it off, because I was doing capital sales with a super long sales cycle, I sold almost nothing my first 6 months on the job. And after six months I was going on 100% commission so I was super stressed.

Talk about wanting to quit! Some days I just wanted to come home, cry, and never go on another sales call. But during that time, I was reminded of one of the best lessons of my life that I actually first learned in college:

The things you think will kill you won't.

And it sounds super simple but a lot of times we're like, "Oh my gosh, I'm gonna die, this is so hard…" And then it's like, "Wait, no, I'm still here."

We can always push ourselves harder than we think we can. Both fighting for something and quitting at something are choices, even when they don't feel like they are.

Too often we beat ourselves up for even wanting to quit. But wanting to quit doesn't make you weak. The most relentless person you know wants to quit sometimes, and has had those days where they didn't push themselves and actually did quit. For each of us the point we'll quit is different, but for all of us, that point gets farther and farther away every day we show up and work hard.

There will be times you'll want to quit but you'll fight through instead. Those are awesome because they mean that you just built more confidence. Reward yourself for those! Celebrate anytime you make the right decision. Positive reinforcement always works.

There will also be times when you don't push through, or that you'll try to push through and you'll fail, and your best still won't be enough. For me, those are the hardest ones, like, "Dang! I tried so hard and it still didn't work!" In those moments I always remember this beautiful quote by Mary Anne Radmacher, that says:

Courage doesn't always roar. Sometimes it's that quiet voice at the end of the day saying, "I will try again tomorrow."

Sometimes the most courageous thing we can do is get up when everything is telling us we can't. In my life, I've fallen down A LOT. I'm sure I'll fall a lot more. And even though sometimes it took a little longer than others, I've always gotten up.

That's the thing: each fall is a chance to find the strength to get up. The cool thing is that once you find that strength, you have it to use for anything else, whenever you need it. It's kind of like you're fear resume.

For a lot of us though, motivation isn't the only issue. There's one question I hear all the time and that's, "How do I know when to quit and when to try harder?" There are some things that are on that line, that we're fighting so hard for but question if it's really worth it. How do we figure that out?

When it comes to this what I've done is to differentiate in my mind between quitting and walking away.

Quitting by definition means to leave somewhere or stop something. So in essence, they're both the same action, just with different connotations.

In my mind, quitting is when you're not willing to do the work required to make it work. Walking away is when the willingness is there, but no matter how hard you work, it won't work.

I had to figure this out my third year in the WNBA when I broke my kneecap in a game. It was the most painful thing I've ever felt. I had to go through seven months of long and painful rehab to get back on the court. But if I had looked at the path ahead or the path I was on at the time and said, "No, that's too hard," I would say that's quitting.

Fast-forward three years. After my broken kneecap, I had torn my Achilles, torn my ACL and then did a bunch of random things to my foot, all while playing basketball. At that point, it wasn't that I wasn't willing to work hard enough but the fact that my body was showing me that no matter what I did, it wasn't going to work. The sacrifices I was making had always been worth it, but at that point, it wasn't anymore. So I decided to walk away.

At the end of the day, I believe the difference between quitting and walking away really comes down to the heart behind the decision.

If you're trying to decide what to do about a given situation, here are a few questions to help you decide when to try harder and when to walk away:

1. Is it making you better even though it's hard? Persevere.
2. Is sentimentality the only thing keeping you there? Walk away.

1. Is it taking you towards the things you said you wanted? Persevere.
2. Is it taking you the opposite direction of the life you want, or not allowing you to pursue it? Walk away.

1. Is the end result more valuable than what you sacrifice along the way? Persevere.
2. Are you sacrificing too much to justify the end result? Walk away.

1. Is there more you can give to see if it will work? Persevere.
2. Is it a situation that won't work no matter how hard you work? Walk away.

1. Are others depending on you as part of a team? Persevere, but if that's

the only reason you'd stay, make arrangements for the future.

2. Is it preventing you from being the person you need to be? Walk away.

You can't walk away if you haven't tried as hard as you can to make it work. That's quitting. Go back and fight for what you want. But there's no point in continuing to work at something that isn't going to lead to what you want. In that case, you need to walk away.

A lot of times we love what we're doing but compatibility is just as important as love. We'll go into this more when we start talking about relationships, but this is just as true in other areas of life. If something isn't compatible with who you are or the life you want, walking away from it isn't just good, it's necessary.

Now for everything we decide to persevere in, there are 3 things that usually keep us from continuing to fight when things get hard:

Guilt, Fear and Fatigue.

Ugh, these three! The best example I can give you in dealing with them myself was in the past when trying to walk away from an unhealthy relationship. I'd promise myself not to call, text, or answer the phone. Then the very next minute I'd be doing exactly what I said I wouldn't. Or swearing we're never going to see each other again. And then two days later we're hanging out.

Each time I had so much guilt that I'd failed (again), fear that I'd just keep failing without ever getting it right, and fatigue from trying to pry my heart away from that person one more time. No matter what you're trying to do, if it's new or difficult, you will have to conquer guilt, fear and fatigue.

So how do we do that?

First of all, guilt is the little, big voice in your head saying, "Coulda, shoulda, woulda." The problem is that it always looks back at what you can't change instead of forward at what you can. And that makes it pointless.

Hear me when I say this: Guilt is a very real feeling that you really need to ignore.

Start from where you are. Life gives us billions of chances to make the right choice. No matter how many times in a row we've made the wrong one, we can always make the next one the right one. Constantly remind yourself to live forward until it becomes a habit, and that voice of guilt will fade into the background.

While guilt is what we feel when we look backward, fear comes once we turn and start looking forward. And we talked about this in chapter one. A lot of times it's the fear that we can't do what's ahead, or maybe the fear of just not knowing what that is. The way to conquer fear is one step at a time.

Remind yourself of the power of one: One decision becomes one action, one after another.

This one is hanging on my wall, written on a giant sheet of paper.

When I made the decision to start my business, I knew two things: that I wanted to help people and that I didn't want to do it working for anyone else. There were so many things I had to figure out, and so many more I didn't know that I didn't know yet. And the fear of those things kept me from making that decision for a long time. I got stuck in that paralyzing space where you don't know how something is going to get done and so you don't start doing it.

The power of one is what helped me get over that. One decision becomes one action, one after another.

I knew I eventually wanted to run my own self-sustaining business. But I put that bigger goal on the shelf because it was too overwhelming. And instead I asked myself, "What would I need to do in order to sell one product?" That was an easy answer: I would need a product. And an easy action: create a product. So I started working on that and took individual steps until I had a product.

Then I asked myself, "How could I tell people about my product?" That was another easy answer: I have to market it. The action wasn't so easy – because I didn't know much about marketing – but one I could figure out or hire out. And it just kept going. Taking one step at a time and figuring things out on the way.

It's how I've accomplished everything else in my life, from becoming a college all American to playing in the WNBA to selling millions and winning awards, even though all of those things had a lot of fear attached to them.

I've heard people say jump off the cliff and grow wings on the way down. But it doesn't always have to be something so extreme. There are cliffs, yes, but most of the things we have to do are more like stairs. We don't necessarily have to jump and fly. We just need to step and walk.

Being able to shift your focus away from your biggest dreams and goals to the small steps needed to accomplish them is how you do anything great.

If you focus on everything you have to do to accomplish your end goal, the distance from where you are to where you're going may scare you, or at least, be overwhelming.

But if you focus on one step, it's only one step. It's only one decision. Look at your goals to remind yourself of the vision, but train yourself to stay and work in each individual moment, while you're in that moment. When you chase progress, you'll always find success.

One thing that I can say about taking steps towards my goals, even when I've been afraid, is that the energy to hope has always been worth the reward. Even when things didn't turn out as planned.

In this case, I'm living my dream of helping people and getting paid for it. Goal in progress. But there have been other goals I haven't met, like becoming an Olympian, having my own TV show (yet), or winning a WNBA Championship.

Still, in every case, the work made me better and built confidence, even despite the disappointment in the result. And that's the way to keep fear from stealing your confidence; one decision becomes one action, one after the other. So what are some small steps that you can take right now towards one of your biggest goals?

After fear comes fatigue. The more you try the more tired you get. Doing the same thing over and over, hoping it'll eventually turn out right is tiring. So is fighting opposition on the way to your goals.

But there is no limit to the amount of times you should try to do what you know you need to.

Never working is the only way to avoid tired. So if you're trying to do anything worth doing, it's going to happen on the way there. But it's ok. Tired won't kill you. And achievement is on the other side!

One of the things I used to do all the time when I was playing is something I started calling "intentional rest." A lot of times in the course of the game, I was aware of being tired and out of breath but I didn't recognize when I was resting. So I started being intentional about resting in moments of rest. Like during a free throw, I'd remind myself, "I'm resting." During a time out or a dead ball, I'd remind myself, "I'm resting." It helped so much!

Now that I'm not playing anymore, I still do this and it still works. I'm super busy so I have to build rest time into my day. And it's really tempting to be on social media or other things that aren't work during your rest time, but you have to realize that as long as your mind is occupied you're not really resting. Intentionally rest – even if it's only for five or ten minutes – and you'll feel more rested. That helps with the tiredness.

Coach Gaudet was one of the best coaches I ever had. He told me something one day in practice that I'll never forget. He said, "The game isn't necessarily always fun. You're getting hit and elbowed, emotions are going up and down, and sometimes your body is so tired you want to stop running.

But what's fun is afterwards, when you've given everything you had, and you can just sit and think to yourself, 'We kicked their butt.'" Remember that afterwards, the work is always worth it.

You can also consult your Confidence Survival Kit that you made in chapter one. That will definitely help you fight guilt, fear and fatigue.

***

Everyone will say you should work hard. But there's one thing that most people forget when they're talking about work, and that's initiative.

Have you ever been driving somewhere, hit a closed road, and been like, "Well, there's no way to get there, I guess I'll go home." No, right? Because of course there's another road! Initiative is like hitting your maps app and finding all the possible ways to get where you're going.

And since we all want to get where we're going – in the car and in life – we're going to talk about two ways to take initiative:

1. The initiative to go above and beyond.
2. The initiative to change something for the better.

With number one – going above and beyond – when I was looking for my first sales job, one piece of advice my recruiter gave me was to leverage every connection. So during my first interview, I asked the guy that would eventually be my boss if there was anyone else I could talk with to learn more about the job. I called both numbers he gave me and at the end of each phone call, I asked them the same question.

By the time the 3-week interview process was over, I had talked to 10 different people within the company about the industry, and my job specifically. After I was hired, my boss told me that several of them had reached out to him on their own and recommended me, not just because of the conversations we had but also because I had taken the initiative to call them even before I was hired.

That's the thing about initiative: When you show you'll do whatever it takes to succeed, people with the same mindset will go out of their way to help you. Because they know how hard it is so they appreciate it.

When we're not willing to take initiative it's usually one of three things:

Laziness – In that case no one can help. You just need to make the decision to work, make it tomorrow, and the next day and keep making it.

We don't really want it – You don't really like your job so you're not willing to go out of your way for it. You don't really like that person so you're not willing to go out of your way for them. And in that case, you need to figure out what you do want and how to get there. Usually, when we're talking about going above and beyond, taking initiative in your current role will open doors to something else you may love. Work wise. Don't apply that to relationships (laughing).

The third reason we don't take initiative is that it's a defense mechanism to protect us. We don't want to invest everything we have because we might be disappointed. This one goes back to the mindset that it's better to do nothing than something that might not work. That's never true! So we have to go back to our positive self-talk, go back to our arguments against fear, and use them! Fight and go for it!

That's the initiative to go above and beyond. The second way to take initiative is to change something that's no longer getting you where you want to go.

Initiative says, "I have everything I need to get everything I need, now how can I use it?" You're already invested so you might as well do everything you can to make it work. This requires a certain mindset. We have to believe that we have the power to change things. So do you?

Do you believe that you have the power to change things in your life?

My job between playing professional basketball and medical device sales was coaching college basketball. I loved certain aspects of it but some things just weren't for me.

I needed to be able to control my own career advancement and location. I needed the freedom to be myself and a healthy work environment. I also needed time to do things outside of work, which is basically a fantasy in the coaching world.

At that point, I had no idea what else I was good at that I could get paid for doing, and I refused to accept the fact that I had to retire from playing at age 29 and hate going to work for the rest of my life.

That's where our decision has to happen. Are we going to continue on a path that isn't getting us what we want because we don't believe we can change it? Are we going to keep settling for things because we don't believe we can do better? Are we going to let our confidence in our ability die a little bit more each day because we're not willing to find another road?

That's like knowing the road is closed and sitting in traffic waiting for them to finish construction and open it back up. Or instead, actually turning around and going home. I just couldn't do it!

Then I met this guy who had left coaching for some other job and he had freedom and money. And I was like, "Dude, what do you do?!" He told me he was in medical device sales so I started to do some research. I found parallels between the recruiting I was already doing as a coach and the job I would be doing as a sales rep.

After doing my research, I put out applications, went through the interview process with a couple med device companies and as they say, the rest is history. I ended up having a great career in med sales before deciding to become an entrepreneur full time and more importantly, I loved it.

But it started by believing I could change a situation that I didn't like. I would've never discovered how well that job fit me by living in the mindset of being stuck where I was.

The first step to changing where you are is to decide you don't belong there.

You may have noticed that I said I NEEDED more freedom, time and a healthy workspace. For me, those things weren't options; they were necessities. If I had to, I would've taken a job with less money for those in return; that's how important they were to me. And because those necessities weren't being fulfilled in my current job, I didn't belong where I was. It was that simple. Once I realized that, I started taking steps to fix it.

So what is it you need in your job, relationships, place of worship or any other area in your life? I'm not talking about wants like, "I want a corner office," or, " I want a girl or guy who looks like this." I'm talking about the things you absolutely need to stay there and continue growing as a whole person.

Sometimes we act like growth is an option. But among the things you get from this book, I hope one is the mindset that your growth in every area of your life is very much a necessity, and also very much in your control.

We have to believe that we have the power to change things. You want to change something? Try. Reject the idea that it is what it is. Ugh, I hate that phrase! I used to say it all the time and I had to stop!

The amazing Pat Summitt once said: "It is what it is. But it will be what you make it."

This is so true! And I think it's important to especially focus on the latter part of that sentence. If you don't like it, change it! If you can't change it, change its role in your life. For me, I couldn't change the requirements of coaching so I had to change my part in it.

We can hope and hope and hope that things change, that they get better. But any hope worth the energy it takes to maintain it has to have action attached.

I will say though, before changing where you are always look at your mindset and attitude FIRST. Because even when your environment changes, the same you is still going to show up there. We have to make sure the problem is where we are and not how we're operating there.

Sometimes we want to leave a situation because of changes we should make but are unwilling to. For example, I was talking to a friend the other day and she said she needed to go into business for herself because she can't work for anyone else. While that's a good thought, there's a difference between can't do and don't want to.

As an entrepreneur, I work for myself. But I can work for someone else because I can get along with different types of people, submit to someone else's authority, help carry out their vision and anything else that needs to be done. I have that ability.

I don't want to work for someone else because I'd rather build my work into my life instead of my life around my work and build my dreams instead of someone else's. But there's a big difference between can't and don't want to.

Dealing with people is a skill that you need. Following directions is a skill that you need. Working hard is a choice that you need to make. If you're not willing to do those where you are, a change of environment isn't going to help because the same you is going to show up and those same problems are going to come with you.

Initiative is important, for work, for success and for confidence. But take the initiative to improve before you take the initiative to leave, in any situation.

And then, if you make the right changes, it'll change where you are into somewhere you want to be or open up doors for you to go somewhere else.

Remember, you are NEVER helpless. Things may be what they are now but they will be whatever you make them. It takes commitment to work!

Step 5
BUILD YOUR TEAM

"Be courteous to all but intimate with few, and let those few be well tried before you give them your confidence."
~ George Washington

Over the next two chapters, we're going to discuss the people in your life. In a nutshell, there are certain types who belong there and others who don't. I doubt you could find anyone to disagree with that. But when talking about cutting people out, one phrase applies more than anything else:

Easier said than done.

You probably already know which people are making you better and which ones are making you worse, and if your decisions were based on that, some people would've been gone a long time ago. But they're not. Your decision to keep them in your life is more than likely based on feelings.

I've been in enough one-sided friendships and complicated relationships to know that feelings don't listen to anyone. I know you're not going to end it until you're ready to, no matter what anyone – including me – says. But that's not going to stop me from trying. So here I go, screaming, "DEATH TO SENTIMENTALITY!" as I write these next several pages.

On the other side of the spectrum is my relationship with my sister, Kristin. The other day I texted her a picture of my hair looking crazy on the way to the hair shop. She responded, "Hahaha. Sooooo cute though!" It was definitely not anyone's kind of cute.

My response: "Only a sister would say that. And with that comment, you have lost all credibility. I can never take your word that I look good in anything, ever again. Haha."

I love my sister, and I know she would tell me I was looking crazy if I actually planned on going anywhere but the hair shop looking the way I was. That's not the point though. It's the fact that for my entire life I've had someone there to unconditionally support who I am and what I do.

I was blessed to have one of those people born into my inner circle. But along the way, we all have to make choices about who fills those other spots. Our confidence level will vary based on how smart we are with those choices.

FACT: You will never be confident if you surround yourself with people who don't want you to be.

To take that a step further, anyone who doesn't actively participate in helping you build confidence should never be a priority in your life. How confident we feel has a lot to do with who we look to for approval and listen to for advice.

When you find people who inspire you to be better without making you feel inadequate as you are, keep them.

Write that down somewhere. Does that statement describe your closest relationships? Anyone else who makes you question whether you're good enough without encouraging and/or helping you be better has got to go.

Is there anyone you know who pops into your mind when you read the following descriptions?

- People who are only happy when you're doing worse than they are.

Being great is hard enough without people trying to keep you average. If they aren't happy with where they are and where they're going, and that unhappiness manifests as trying to tear you down instead of walk with you, they have to go.

- People who are only around when things are good. The minute you can't give them what they want, be it money, status, sex, fun, or whatever else, they peace out. Let them leave and don't make the mistake of giving them the chance to do it again without evidence of a serious change of heart on their part.

- People who point out your flaws without acknowledging the great things about you. They have to go. Most of us are already super hard on ourselves without others cosigning our negative self-talk.

- People who make you feel like you're not worth their time, every time. You are absolutely worth someone's time. It's just going to take someone ELSE to see that. Stop asking for their time and quit giving them yours.

- And then there's those people – or that person – you know you need to let go of, and you've known that for a while, but just haven't done it yet. We talked about them at the start of this chapter. Maybe they're still there because even though they treat you like crap, you still love them. Or because they make you feel something when you're with them that you don't feel by yourself. Maybe they're exactly what you need in one area of your life and not at all what you need in another. There can be a lot of reasons and not every relationship is black and white in terms of good and bad. I'm not saying your relationship has to be perfect because none of them are. All relationships are work, but if they're complicated, you're working on the wrong ones. Let them go so you can find what you need somewhere else. I realize that it may be hard to believe healthy, uncomplicated relationships exist, especially if you've never seen one. If that's the case, this is one instance where you need to dream bigger than your surroundings.

Think about the names that came to mind as you were reading through that list. Do any of them surprise you? They might just be people you need to have honest conversations with about how you're feeling.

If they came up then obviously there's some hidden issue there. Maybe it's something you can work through and continue to be close. But if you express how you feel, or have already time and time again, and they still don't change, it's time to start putting some distance between you and them for the sake of your confidence.

One of my favorite quotes from Gandhi says:

"I will not let you walk through my mind with your dirty feet."

Let's say you just put brand new carpet in your house and one of your friends comes to the door with mud-covered shoes. Are you going to invite her in and let her walk through the house without getting cleaned up first? If so you're a better friend than me!

My friend is going to have two options: we can either talk outside or she can take her shoes off and come inside. Am I wrong for that? No. Because it's my house and my responsibility to keep it clean.

How much more important is your life than your carpet?

We should all meet people where they are because they're never going to be perfect and neither are we. That's what answering the door is. But the level of access they have to your life has to correspond with where they are in theirs. It's ok to help them get cleaned up if you want. That doesn't mean letting them in the door before they do. And if they start getting you filthy as you're helping, you may need to take a step back and let them do it on their own.

The problem is that as soon as we start limiting who's in our lives because of the dirt they have in their lives, people start throwing around the "J word." You know... judgment. Sigh. Please understand that it's not judgmental to assess a situation based on what you see and decide if it's good for you or not. It's called discernment.

Discernment: The ability to see and understand people, things or situations clearly and intelligently.

The key word in this definition is "clearly." Judgment, in this context, is when your own assumptions, prejudices or previous experiences prevent you from seeing a situation or person CLEARLY. Judgment will negatively influence your actions in that situation or towards that person.

Discernment, on the other hand, is using the evidence to see that same situation or person CLEARLY, and then acting accordingly. It's discerning to control who has access to your life based on the potential impact they have on it.

Everyone is not entitled to your time.

Controlling access doesn't mean you go and start demanding things from your friends. I don't demand anything from the people I give my time and effort to. If they're going to stay in my life though, there are certain requirements. We get in trouble when we start treating our time like a right instead of a privilege.

You don't have to be rude about cutting people out of your life either. Just start putting a little distance between you and them in terms of time spent and effort invested. You may still be able to be cool without keeping them close. It depends on the relationship. Be nice, smile, encourage them and treat them with respect, as you would anyone else.

At the end of the day though, you don't have to open up to them, treat them as a friend or go running to their rescue every time they need something. Set and maintain whatever boundaries you need to in order to move forward.

Side note: This does not put a limit on forgiveness. If someone is genuinely interested in changing, give him small opportunities to show you. Not tell you. SHOW you.

Trust them enough to let them prove you can trust them again.

So commit to an action with each person you thought of while reading this chapter. Now this might be easy in some relationships, those people who all you need to do is have a conversation with them, or the ones you're ready to let go of anyway.

But this is going to be really hard for others; those people you aren't ready to let go but know you need to. I personally think the best way to do this is quit cold turkey, but it's also the hardest. Relationships are like drugs in that it's going to get worse before it gets better. But the longer you wait, the more time you waste and it's never going to get any easier. If you're not willing to commit to cold turkey yet, it's ok.

Make your goals small and attainable. If you text every morning, wait until lunch. Or if you spend every night with that person, start planning fun things to do with other friends. A lot of time it's breaking the habit of what you're used to as much as it is breaking away from the actual person.

Commit to taking steps in your relationships that are going to help you build that confidence you want in the long run.

***

We talked about who we shouldn't keep close, but who are the ones we should? When I'm talking about these people I call them the Inner Circle.

THE INNER CIRCLE: A group of people you can let close enough to hurt you because you know they would never do it intentionally.

We're all human, and because of that, we will hurt each other. But your Inner Circle of people, the ones you intentionally keep around you, won't do it on purpose.

None of us were meant to walk through life alone. We all need people to share the journey with, and friends to make hilarious, exciting memories with, who will be there during the hardest times too.

But we have to be careful of the type of people we keep in our circle be-cause no matter how strong you are, we're all vulnerable when we let people close.

I had to learn this the hard way. I never started out as the popular girl. In high school people knew who I was because I was an athlete but I didn't have many friends to call on a Friday night if I was bored.

So when I got to college, I decided I wanted to be "cool" for the first time. I started going out all the time – partying, flirting and dating – all so I could make as many "friends" as possible. And it continued all the way into my years playing professionally.

I loved having so many social options. We'd all go out and get crazy together. And I didn't feel like I needed to be extra selective about who I talked to or confided in or trusted. It was awesome!

Right up until the messiness that comes from doing private things with public people. That's when I figured out that "good" is always better than "a lot."

Quality relationships with a few are better than superficial interactions with a lot.

Think of the phrase, "What happens in Vegas stays in Vegas." That's only true if you go with people who won't get anything from telling everyone else what happened. Some people don't have a compass that defines what they should and shouldn't do in relationships. And even if they do, it might be different than yours!

And that's the situation I found myself in. I found out quickly that every person I called a friend was not the kind of friend I needed. That's a lesson I never forgot.

Once we learn that lesson though, we can be tempted not to trust anyone, and to put up walls to keep ourselves from getting hurt. When we start feeling like that, we have to remind ourselves where the real problem is.

Trusting is strength in character. Trusting the wrong people is weakness in judgment.

So as we're talking about changing the dynamics of your relationships, if you find yourself really hesitant to trust, start looking at your discernment and your ability to see people clearly instead of pulling back your trust all together.

We all need someone we can get crazy with, stupid silly with, or break down to. But you have to be careful in choosing who that is. True friends won't base their complete opinion of you on the limited view of a night, week or month. They don't spread all your business around and they understand that you're not weak for having a moment of weakness. Most of all, they would never use any of that against you.

Sometimes people look at me and think I never struggle. Which couldn't be farther from the truth. It's not that I never struggle. They're just not the ones I show, and the ones I do aren't telling anyone! We all have to make sure the people closest to us prove they can handle that role correctly before we give it to them.

There is a difference between associates and friends. You network and hang out with associates and the more you have, the easier it is to get things done. It's like a friendly connection without all the deep, emotional stuff. Make associates.

But you experience life with friends. They're the ones who are there no matter what you need and when you need it, and you can honestly say that you'd do the same for them.

Friends aren't made. Through shared experiences they kind of just happen. Because it's not that you can't do what you want. It's just that sometimes, you shouldn't be doing it with the people who were there.

Vulnerability isn't weakness until you show it to someone who uses it against you. And being selective about what you show people outside of your inner circle doesn't make you fake. It makes you smart.

So now as we go through a few types of people I want you to pay attention to any names that come to mind for each description. Ready?

PEOPLE IN your Inner Circle…

1. Accept you for you
Sometimes we feel like we have to try. Try to be cooler, try to be smarter, or try to be better to impress "people." The people you should keep close are those who you don't have to try to be anything with. You can just be you – whoever that is – at any given moment, even during the figuring out process.

2. Add positivity to your life
Positive people aren't always happy and negative people aren't always sad. But there is a huge difference in their energy. It's much better to be around someone who gives you energy instead of weighing you down with the weight of drama or chronic unhappiness.

3. Inspire you to be a better person
They don't make you feel like you need to be a different person to be good enough, but they do inspire you to be a better version of yourself. Those people are rare so if you find any, value them.

4. Will be there for you, even when it's inconvenient
Being friends when things are easy doesn't really prove anything. But when everyone else turns their backs on you, who's still there, refusing to let

you quit? Who's still there refusing to quit on you? Those are the important people. No one else really matters.

5. Will be honest with you, no matter what

Good friends are genuine. You can trust who they show you because it's who they are. Their words match their actions match their lives. Inner circle friends will have your back but will also get in your face when needed. And that person in your face is only there because they want the best for you.

Based on this list, can you think of anyone whose role in your life needs to change? What about that person who has some of these characteristics but you haven't spent as much time building that relationship? What could you do to change that?

You'll notice that these are all character traits. We need to challenge ourselves not to put too much emphasis on appearance, money or status when it comes to choosing friends. Those things may help as different situations come up, but they're not as important as character when building solid relationships.

If someone has certain traits like looks, money or status, they may be a great fit for the associates pile, but without these character traits, I don't care who they are, they don't belong in the friend pile.

At the end of the day, who a person is matters more than what they have because who they are will attract what they deserve.

So go through your friends list. For each person, ask yourself, "Does he or she have a positive impact on my life?" "Which of the previous lists does he or she belong on?"

In general, who are the most positive people you know? Are they the ones you spend the most time with? As you start to answer these questions, you'll know who to move forward with and who may need to be on the associate level.

Also, if you're not the type of friend I just described, you either won't attract those people or won't be able to keep them once you do. So which needs to change: the way you show friendship or the friends you choose?

The team you build around you will be the first line of attack against you or the first line of defense for you. Your choices determine which role they play. Remember it's impossible to be confident if you're surrounded by people who don't want you do be, so choose wisely!

Step 6
DEFINE YOUR STANDARD
"Love is always more than words and bigger than feelings."

Isn't it crazy how a close relationship can swing your confidence level from one extreme to another overnight? And by close I mean those who have an immediate impact on your life, like your supervisor, best friend or significant other.

Seriously, one of the best things about a healthy relationship is its unconditional acceptance. When someone we're close to supports who we are and what we do, confidence just seems to flow.

In the same way, one of the worst things about an unhealthy relationship is that it's impossible to find steady confidence while in one. If someone we're close to is emotionally or mentally unsupportive, our ability to be confident will be hidden behind our ties to that person.

A lot of times, the types of relationships we have with other people stem equally as much from our definition of two things as it does who the other person actually is. And those two things are respect and love.

So how do we define them?

Merriam-Webster defines respect as an act of giving special attention or high regard.

And it defines love as a strong affection for a person, attraction based on sexual desire, or a warm attachment, enthusiasm and devotion.

Is that how you define them? Probably a better question is what are the practical definitions for respect and love? What do they look like in practice?

It's so important to define both respect and love for ourselves because if we don't know what something actually is, it's really easy to accept imitations of it.

I personally think the dictionary definition of love is terrible because it's ambiguous, not at all in depth and doesn't really tell us how to live it out. And respect is a little better but still not practical.

Some words I would use to define love for myself are loyal, considerate, wants the best for me, not intentionally hurtful, not secretive, forgiving and protective.

For respect, my definition is "treats me as valuable." Pretty simple on that one!

Does that sound closer to your definitions than Webster's?

We talked about that first because our definition of love and respect are our first and most important standards, and will set the bar for every other standard in our lives.

Standard is defined as, "a level of quality or attainment."

Relationships are a lot of give and take, yes's and no's. You and your significant other will never agree on everything, and you have to be flexible. And you and your supervisor probably won't agree on everything either but she's still your boss.

Certain things, however, should not be up for discussion. And the standards you set relate directly to whether or not that person's action contradicts your definition of respect and love, depending on which is appropriate for that relationship.

I call this my list of non-negotiables. For example:

Professionally, meeting times, deadlines and office space are some things that are negotiable or tolerable, because they won't interfere with my definition of respect, under normal circumstances.

In my personal relationships, where we eat at or what movie we see is negotiable because under normal circumstances, neither of them would contradict my definition of love and so it's ok to compromise on them. Makes sense right?

Now when things start to compromise your definition of respect or love, they go on the non-negotiable list. For example:

Professionally, me being talked to like a valuable person or paid what I'm worth is non-negotiable. Because there's no way I would ever feel respected if my coworkers talked to me any kind of way or I know that I'm getting paid less than someone else doing the same work.

Personally, being in an exclusive relationship and supporting my dreams is non-negotiable because those things are necessary for me to feel loved.

Loyalty is part of my definition of love and so I know I could never be confident if my heart belonged to someone whose actions were telling my I'm not enough to own his.

I think as women, that's how we get the reputation for being crazy. By allowing ourselves to get in situations that will drive us there because we think we can control our emotions after handing them over to someone else.

The key to getting your non-negotiables is being willing to walk away if you don't. Don't bluff because without follow through, that "standard" is just a good idea.

Unfortunately your feelings usually care nothing about your standards.

That makes it hard to wait on compatibility when a love-look-alike is standing right in front of you. Or leave a job that feels secure even though you hate it and aren't treated well.

On the relationship side, someone who can't meet your standards may even love you the best way he knows how. But the best way he knows how can still break you, if his definition of love is different than yours.

Professionally, just because it's a good job, doesn't mean it's a good fit.

Respect yourself more than you like or love anyone. And even when you don't feel like you do, act like you do first. Your heart will follow your feet and the standard you set is the standard you get.

Don't be mean about it or make some ridiculous list that's impossible for any one person to live up to. Or expect things professionally that are unrealistic for your experience. That's how people end up unemployed and single forever.

Just figure out exactly what you need to feel safe and satisfied. No reason to demand anything.

The right person will make sure you feel safe and respected, work or personally. If he or she doesn't want that, it's not the right fit.

Many of us have been in a relationship at some point where we let feelings get in the way of standards.

A few years back I was in a relationship with a guy. I thought he was amazing. I was excited by his success, ambition and the way we mentally connected.

So when problems with honesty and faithfulness started showing up, I brushed them off. First I told myself they were nothing. Then I told myself I could live with them, immediately followed by my decision that I could fix him. I didn't rationalize because I really believed him. I did it because I wanted to believe him.

So I started trying to "help" him and we talked through it each time something he said or did didn't quite add up. I listened to all of his explanations, hoping and waiting for him to act like the man he said he wanted to be.

The only thing worse than him lying to you is you lying to yourself so you can believe him.

And I did lie to myself for a few months. Until I got a random call and Facebook messages from his "ex" with pictures that made it impossible to continue.

I was so mad. Not at her. After all, I couldn't blame her for his choices and if she was still coming around it was because he wanted her around. No, I was pissed at him.

But in the back of my mind, the knowledge had already been there without the willingness to believe it. So how mad at him could I really be?

You can't blame someone for what you continuously allow.

So many of us are inspired to fix the beautiful disasters, whether it's in a relationship or at a job. The reality is, you can't fix anyone if they're breaking you in the process. Remember the mud on the carpet example from the last chapter?

I know it's hard. But sometimes the hardest thing and the right thing are the same thing. The standards of love and respect that you set have to become the ones you're not willing to compromise.

As you set your list of non-negotiables remember they're the things that are absolutely necessary for any relationship you're in because otherwise you'd be compromising your definitions of love and respect.

Make sure they're things you're willing to stick to, because if you don't, they were just good ideas.

Also, on the relationship side, make sure it's not some ridiculous list that no one but Jesus could live up to. We are all flawed people, so don't paint a picture of the perfect man or woman. Paint a picture of someone you can love and live with, who will love you in return.

***

People always want to talk about the mushy, touchy-feely side of love. But love without compatibility will drive you crazy.

The story always goes the same. We meet someone who we're instantly drawn to in a way we can't resist. Of course no attraction like that could happen with anyone who wasn't perfect for us.

So we jump in, heart first, and fall in love with the way the world stops whenever we're both breathing the same air.

That description makes me laugh because that's how all my relationships used to start…ha. But there's a huge catch. Yes, I know it's amazing, but the catch is you don't really know that person. And that may seem kind of obvious but we forget it a lot. We're all caught up in chemistry and vibe.

But chemistry can't replace their character and the vibe y'all share can't replace the honesty they haven't had to prove yet.

So now your heart is set on someone who may very well turn out to be crazy or abusive or just not a good fit for whatever reason, despite the fact that they "feel" perfect. Chemistry is a necessity but compatibility is what makes relationships work.

You will meet thousands of people in your life. Some of them aren't worth your time, some can't handle who you are, and some just aren't ready to give what you need. That doesn't mean they're bad people or that being with them wouldn't feel great. But it does mean that they don't fit into your life in the form of a significant relationship.

Pain comes when we allow people to play roles in our lives that they are not properly equipped to play.

It's like a puzzle. All the pieces look pretty together because they have the same coloring and may look like abstract art. But only the right piece fits together. I've found that people will naturally fall into the role that fits them. If you have to force them into a place in your life, they're probably not meant to be there. Like trying to fit a square peg into a round hole.

It's nearly impossible to be confident when you're in pain and the source of that pain is constantly renewing itself because you're trying to force something that doesn't fit.

What does compatibility look like? It's when he makes you better, you make him better and your strengths balance out each other's weaknesses. You don't have to be walking the exact same path but you do need to be going the same direction.

It doesn't mean everything is easy and perfect. It just means that you don't have to deny something that's fundamentally you to be with that person.

Like if you want to be a mom and he never wants kids or if one of you has kids and the other doesn't want to raise someone else's kids, you're not compatible.

If he wants a housewife and giving up your career sounds like hell to you, you're not compatible.

Or a big one is if your values are different. For example, if you think love includes monogamy and he doesn't, you're not compatible.

Now obviously relationships are full of compromises. But you don't want to feel like you're compromising the foundations and ideals of who you are.

Compatibility means that if you turned your feelings off, that person would still fit into your life and improve it.

If you're wondering if you're compatible with someone or not, two of the easiest ways to tell are:

- If you fight over dumb stuff. Every time you get into an argument, afterwards you're like, "Huh? How the heck did that happen?" Or, "Why were we even talking about that?" That probably means you're not compatible.

- You're always disagreeing about the same thing, over and over. Or if you feel like there are certain topics you're always pushing under the rug instead of talking about it. That may be a clue that it's goes beyond just a disagreement and is more of a value difference. And in that case you're not compatible.

A lot of times people say that love is enough. And that's almost true. It's mostly enough.

Love is the feeling that makes it all worth it and then the commitment to keep it there. It separates the business partners from the friends from the spouses. But compatibility is what separates the "ex" from the "forever." It's usually not love.

***

True, visible confidence comes from inside, so it'll always be directly influenced by the condition of your heart. And that's why you have to guard it.

Above all else, guard your heart, for everything you do flows from it.
~ Proverbs 4:23

Now no matter how you feel about the Bible, if you've ever had a broken heart, you know this is absolutely true!

Think about your house. When you leave in the morning you close and lock your door, right? I know I do, so that any random person can't just come in and do whatever they want.

If I do meet someone I think is cool, I'm not going to be like, "Hey, come over!" I'm going to invite them to lunch or to hang out with some friends so I can get to know them and make sure I actually want them in my personal space. That's only smart, right? Most importantly, if I see any signs that make me wonder, I'm not even telling them where I live.

But do we always treat our hearts with that same caution?

Short answer: No. Too often we meet someone who looks good or is successful or makes us feel those little butterflies and suddenly we're caught up before we know their ambitions for the next few months, or even what they've been doing for the last few. We leave the door to our hearts unlocked and invite in any stranger who knocks.

But why be so reckless when you only get one? Wounds of the heart can't be fixed, only healed from. So we need to treat it with more caution than things we can replace with a trip to the store.

One of the side effects of not guarding your heart is that it's hard to know how to act in relationships afterwards. Am I the only one who has let the wrong person in, gotten hurt, and then promised myself to never let anyone in, ever again? Possibly, but I doubt it.

You try your hardest to keep people out but that doesn't really work because none of us were meant to go through this life alone. We're not made like that. So you end up trying to let someone half way in because you don't want to get hurt, don't want to be lonely, but aren't willing to wait for the person who can prove they're trustworthy.

That's like trying to lock all your valuables in a room so that you can invite thieves to a house party. The problem is, once you let them in, they're free to roam; the locks to the doors in our hearts are terrible! They end up getting into the room you tried to lock and of course something always gets stolen.

Then you're hurt and mad. But let's be honest, you knew they were a thief and chose to entertain them anyway. Or weren't willing to wait long enough to find out if they were a thief or not.

Stop it. Quit gambling with your heart because you're unwilling to wait on someone to prove they can be trusted with it.

It's easy to blame the thief, but what about the owner of the house who ignored all evidence and knowingly let him in?

And I'm not just talking about romantic relationships here. This includes friends. Those friends who talk about other friends behind their backs, are always in some kind of drama, or aren't really trying to better themselves. We see the evidence but let them stay close anyway. We have to take better care of our belongings and ourselves.

Guarding your heart also involves being rational. When it comes to relationships, our feelings have an IQ of ZERO. They're super dumb. So we need to think before automatically doing whatever they tell us to.

Stop letting your heart get drunk off feelings caused by people who are only in your life because of your impatience.

You're not doing yourself any good. Be intentional about reminding yourself of the difference between feelings and facts. Do it often regarding your conversations with yourself and with others.

When my relationship a few years back didn't work out. I automatically started asking myself, "How did I mess up this time?" and, "Was it because of something I couldn't give?"

When I complained to my best guy friend about being newly single and how obviously I was doing something wrong, he laughed at me - a little too hard. Then he said, "One woman will never be enough for a guy who wants two." Ha, gotta love the honesty.

Then it sunk in: What they do isn't always because of something I'm not.

People make their own decisions and bottom line is that sometimes that choice is not about you! Reminding yourself of that frees you from feeling like you're not good enough, or getting totally depressed over someone who wasn't even capable of giving you what you needed in the first place.

Think rationally about these situations BEFORE your feelings get all caught up. There's a difference between disappointed and broken. Using your head to guard your heart will stop the process at disappointment before giving it the chance to break you.

I actually had to apply this to my life just the other day. One of my friends introduced me to this guy who was tall, dark and handsome (can I add funny too?). A pretty good start, in my world. We started texting and talked on the phone a couple times, and pretty quickly, I realized that he was someone I could be interested in who was also interested in me.

The problem was, regardless of what I wanted or any possible interest, his relationship with God was non-existent, and that's kinda sorta my first non-negotiable. And you know how us girls do, letting what we want carry our imaginations farther than we should.

So I told him that God was a big deal in my world and that I didn't really build friendships with guys who weren't on the same page. When he said he wasn't interested in that at all, I stopped talking to him on the phone and tried to stop allowing my thoughts to drift and then stay on what he might be doing during the day (that's always the hardest part).

That may seem extreme to some, but I did it to leave my feelings at the very beginning of the road I had found them on. It was my way of guarding my heart, and his heart too.

The best way to live by your standards is not to tempt yourself with things that will compromise them.

Please hear me when I say this:

I'm not telling you to build a fortress around your heart and never let anyone in. I'm also not telling you to make people jump through ridiculous hoops trying to win your approval.

I'm just saying there's no reason to start venturing off into daydreams of your happily ever after, or seriously entertaining someone, without evaluating his ability to be what you need him to be, in the role you want him to play.

If someone has already shown he or she won't be responsible with your heart, stop believing your feelings over the facts. Because when that person acts in line with those facts, it'll cue that inner monologue about you being unlovable and let it run away with your confidence.

When someone shows you who they are, believe them. ~ Oprah

I know it's not really fun to stop entertaining people who aren't what you need. I used to stay playing with fire in relationships. The thrill of trying to make someone who's unattainable fall for you and then the flattery when it actually happens is such a rush.

But at some point, playing with fire burns all of us. One of the most painful times for me was a few years ago when I ended up breaking my own heart and the heart of someone I loved. Trust me when I say that hurt more than the game entertained.

That's why we have to be smart before we're emotional. Being smart in our actions makes it easier to be disciplined with our thoughts. Capture every thought and make it productive, positive, and confident.

Don't be reckless with your heart by giving any and everyone the power to break it. That way, when you do meet someone who deserves it, you can fall in love with that person instead of falling in love with the idea of falling in love. Until then, use your head to guard your heart.

***

Ok we talked about the rational side of having standards, why they're important and how to stick to them.

If it was that easy, we'd all do it. There's one aspect that gets in the way: the emotional side of having standards – the fact that it's freakin' hard, especially when someone you want isn't living up to the standard you set.

And in this section I'm talking to those of us who are prone to unhealthy relationships. That was definitely me and so I know the feeling well. If that's not you, pass this advice on to the friend who needs it because you know we all have one.

One of the standards that helped me break the pattern of unhealthy relationships was to prioritize trust above love. If I can't trust someone, my feeling of love for him doesn't matter.

These days in my relationships, consistency earns trust and trust is the only currency I value.

Once someone earns trust, love is then an option. Unfortunately, what he wants and what he's earned are sometimes two different things. But he'll always take what you give him. That part is completely in your control.

So if he treats you a certain way it's not because he thinks you deserve it, or even because he thinks it's right. He'll treat you that way because he doesn't think you're strong enough to walk away, because you continue to allow it.

In some cases, there's a misunderstanding. If he didn't know what he was doing would hurt you, cool. Talk about it, forgive and move on.

That's not always it though. Sometimes he already knew it'd hurt you but chose to show blatant disregard for your feelings, your relationship, or both. He didn't value your feelings when he did it, and nothing you say now will change that.

You'll keep standing there complaining about what he does if you keep standing there.

Move. Let him do what he's obviously going to do anyway in a way that won't crush your feelings every time. He might be what you want but unless you're out there doing the same things he's doing, he's not what you deserve.

Once you walk away, keep walking. There's no reason to put yourself in a situation to revive old connections when circumstances haven't changed.

If you do go back, I understand. I've done it and many of us have. But don't give up on yourself. Keep trying to do what you know you need to. Take courage and try again.

Sometimes they're meant to be a Once Upon A Time instead of a Happily Ever After.

Maybe you're hoping he'll change while waiting for the right time to leave. It will never feel like a good time. Your love for him and the control he has over you won't change until you make up your mind to change the situation first.

Even when you don't think you can live without him, you can. And even though you don't want to now, you will. Because neither of you is what the other needs.

He needs a girl who will convince herself she's ok with his actions (translated: not you). And you need a guy who won't throw you away every time he walks out the door.

I know having standards isn't always easy. Another gem from my best guy friend was, "A girl can be beautiful, smart, and have great morals. Problem is, there are five girls standing across the street that look just as good as she does and will do anything for his attention. The guy may want the good girl, but sometimes he's going to take the easy way out."

That's so true! There'll be at least one guy (or a few) who chooses not to date you because of what another girl will allow. There will always be "that girl" who gets attention just because of what she'll do for it. And it sucks when you're interested in a guy but he chooses that girl instead. It can definitely wreck your confidence if you let it.

Then you'll be like, "But Chantelle, I'm lonely! I just want a man like everyone else…" Loneliness will have you thinking crazy like, "Why not be 'that girl'?"

And trust me when I say, I totally understand. Nights get long, your phone messages get dry and suddenly being that easy girl across the street with the man starts looking better than being the single girl with standards. Yep, been there.

But loneliness is a feeling and the same as any other feeling, sometimes you have to tell it to shut up.

Sometimes you have to feel lonely to find happy.

There's a big difference between lonely and alone. Lonely feels like there's something missing and whether you're by yourself or with someone else, you're not content. There's no peace in being lonely; instead it feels like there's a hole that needs to be filled.

When you're alone, you are by yourself, and though you might not necessarily want to be, you're content with it. A hole doesn't need to be filled but something else could definitely be added.

The transition from lonely to alone needs to be made while you're single and unoccupied. Because if you can't enjoy your own company, you won't expect others to enjoy it without getting something in return.

You'll also be much less confident in waiting for someone who does, or leaving someone who doesn't.

So how do sex and standards go together? Here's my take on it. There's a huge difference between being the girl he would sleep with and the girl he gets to sleep with.

The one he would sleep with is that girl who is cool chillin' with the guys but knows she's not one of them. She's confident and fun, and pretty, beautiful even, but not so sexy that it's distracting. Her standards make her the friend because he knows if he wants sex, it would have to be a lot more than casual with a "return to chillin' with the boys" mindset.

The girl he gets to sleep with may be the chick he only calls when he wants some. That's the easy girl to judge. But she could also be the same girl I just described with one piece missing: standards. She's that great girl who doesn't enforce her worth.

She settles for being that hook up friend and acting like nothing changed when that's not really what she wants. Or maybe it is what she wants. Either way, whether it's not making him commit to a real relationship, or not treating herself as more than casual, standards are definitely missing.

Any woman can get a man's attention naked. Don't act like that's an accomplishment.

Real skills are getting him with your clothes on, without talking about things you'll do with them off. Until you can do that, chill and keep working on you. Because if he picks the girl with no standards, it's not that you're not good enough. It's that he's too easily impressed. Remind yourself of this and it'll be easier to wait for the right kind of attention instead of being thirsty for the wrong kind.

Stop using sex as a bribe for love.

One thing that supports you in holding to your standards is your definition of sex. Sometimes we see sex as just fun, or as a way to get something, like love or a relationship, from someone.

If it's only fun, that doesn't imply any requirements. If it's a way to get something, that puts the pressure on you to earn whatever you're trying to get in return.

But what if, instead of looking at sex as a good time or a way to earn someone's approval, you saw it as giving yourself away to him? Giving you, and everything you are, to that person to have and do whatever they wanted with?

If sex means you're giving that person something, it puts the pressure back on him. It implies the question, "Did he earn whatever I'm giving him?"

Of course sex is a good time, and surely about the other person too, but those are details. The truth underneath the details is that after you have sex, that person owns part of you. And when they leave, they will take it with them.

That's why it's so much harder not to snap and go crazy over someone you've had sex with. The part of you they own desperately wants to stay with the rest of you.

Unfortunately, that's no longer up to you.
That person determines whether or not you stay whole.

I'm not saying never have sex, obviously. But how many pieces of yourself can you give away before you start feeling like less?

When your definition of sex steers you towards that conversation with yourself, it's a lot easier to set your standards a little higher and then uphold them. Make someone meet your standard before giving him the rewards of the position it earns.

When you find someone who genuinely enjoys you for you and is willing to prove it through his actions, you can do what you do because of how you feel towards him, not because of how you want him to feel towards you.

So the entire point of this discussion is to say that you decide what your relationships look like and what they don't by what you allow and what you won't. Not easy, but simple. And if you're in a situation that this applies to, it's time to start making some decisions.

The last thing we need to remember about our standards is that they aren't just for other people.

When you set standards for the people in your life, ask yourself a few questions:

Do I meet the standard I've set for them?

If I want an honest person, am I honest?

If I want someone who doesn't play games, am I prepared to operate in a relationship without playing games?

If I want someone who is making money, am I doing what I have to do to increase the value I bring to the relationship?

If I want a man of God, am I a woman of God and do my actions match that description?

Provide what you expect.

It makes no sense to set standards for someone else that you're not willing to meet yourself. You'll always attract what you deserve if you're willing to wait for it. But the person you want is also looking for the person they want.

Are you preparing yourself to be that person?

Becoming a better version of you is important for your life and confidence, but let's not pretend that other people won't notice and appreciate the improvement. Do it for you and for those future relationships that will add the right things to your life.

First respect, then trust, then love.

Quality relationships are built in that order. Without the first two, true love doesn't exist. And love without compatibility is the most unproductive thing you can do.

I've had enough crazy and amazing relationships to write an entire book on the "dos" and "don'ts" of them...maybe next time.

For now, set your mind on your standards and use them to guard your heart. Everything, including confidence, comes from there. And when you find someone who is worth taking the risk, go for it and don't look back!

Step 7

UNPACK YOUR HEART

"Charisma comes from public self-acceptance."

Please read this entire section before acting on any of it.

That was in bold for a reason... I'm just saying!

I've moved 32 times in my life. Going somewhere new always makes life feel like the adventure it is. What I've learned is that no matter where I'm moving to, the packing and unpacking part always sucks.

I hate organizing everything into boxes so it'll be easier to figure out where it all goes in the new place. So I usually just throw things anywhere they'll fit with the hope of organizing later.

After I move in, sometimes it takes me months to unpack all the boxes because I either don't need the stuff right away or am just too lazy to get it all done at once. But even though it always takes longer than I'd like, once everything is finally unpacked and put in its place, I feel so much better. I can finally relax and even invite people over.

So what does this whole moving and unpacking concept have to do with your confidence?

Well, I bet you have boxes of experiences and feelings packed away in your head and heart somewhere. You probably stuck them there because you didn't have the time, energy or willingness to figure out exactly what to do with them and where they should go. Surely I'm not the only one who does that, right?

The skill of compartmentalization is useful because it allows us to continue on when certain areas of our lives may be falling apart. Since there also never seems to be a good time to unpack all those feelings, it's really easy to forget where the boxes are. Sometimes we can forget the fact that they exist all together. Or remember and just not feel like dealing with it.

Just because you don't feel the feelings doesn't mean they're not there.

Story of my life! Nothing simply up and disappears. It just means you haven't yet had the luxury of entertaining those feelings and so you probably stuffed them away somewhere.

But just like moving, we'll never feel completely comfortable with ourselves, and especially comfortable enough to wholly share ourselves with others, until we start unpacking.

The more things that are unpacked and put away, the more ready we are for visitors. That makes the process crucial to our wellbeing and ultimately, our confidence. Unpacking is never fun, but if you want to move, you have to do it.

But how do we unpack?

I've learned that this one is probably the hardest step of all and definitely a gradual process. You have to find and address the root of why you don't feel good enough in every area those feelings exist.

For example, I don't struggle with confidence in my ability to connect with people or strategize on how to make things happen. In that area I just need to keep building my "personal resume" so I always have new things to refer to in moments I may question it.

Sometimes, though, it's hard for me to have confidence in the fact that I deserve the best. So that's an area I've had to dig deep in. And that was a whole lot of unpacking!

I can't tell you what your reason is or the root behind it. I can't even tell you where to start looking. What I do know is that you can do everything to make yourself feel better on the outside, but without unpacking your feelings and addressing them, you'll never feel truly confident on the inside.

To get the right answers, we have to ask the right questions. Where? What? Why? How?

Unpacking is a question and answer process you go through with yourself. Where to start depends on your answers. So ask the "where" questions:

Is there anything I have unresolved feelings about?

Is there any part of my thoughts or experiences that I purposely skip over and don't think about?

When did I start questioning myself and/or my worth?
Ask these questions of yourself so that you can find your area of focus.

These answers can lead you anywhere from a job that didn't work out to a past relationship to something from childhood.

If more than one thing comes up, pick one to go through this exercise with and leave the other ones alone. I'll tell you more on why later.

My example: When I started asking myself these questions years ago, one thing that came up was my relationship with my Mom.

What?

Once you find an area of focus, ask "what"?
What happened?
What do I feel about it?
What is the situation now?
The "what" questions will get you the facts.
The "what" questions will get you the facts. They'll tell you what happened to flag this specific situation in your mind as one needed to address.

My example: The relationship between my Mom and I was abusive. It made me feel like I deserved all the bad things that happened to me and that I was less valuable because of it. I also felt angry and resentful towards my Mom for her role in it.

What's your example?

Why?

Asking the "what" questions gets you started. But you won't see the real progress until you go beyond knowing to understanding. That comes from asking the "why" questions.

Why did it happen? Was it because of who I am or because of who someone else is?

Why do I feel this way? Is it because I failed at something I haven't let go of or am blaming myself for something I can't change?

Why can't I get past this? Is this a mindset issue, a heart issue or a situation issue?

My example: I had to realize that what happened had nothing to do with who I was. It was all because of who she was and the situation I'd been placed in. My feelings were the result of me blaming myself for something that wasn't my fault. I was being unfair to me!

I also realized that my Mom didn't have complete control over who she was either. She had an illness that limited her control, and so my anger at her was misplaced; she couldn't help who she was.

The more I put myself in her shoes, I began to feel compassion for her instead of anger. While I didn't have anything to do with the situation I'd been put in, at least I could control who I was and who I became afterward. I could fight for myself. That was an ability my Mom didn't have.

Man, this one was a process as you can see! It took hours of soul-searching and rational thinking to come up with what I just wrote in those paragraphs. It lead to me calling her, trying to learn more about who she was, and trying to build that relationship from the ground up just like I was doing with my confidence.

What realizations come from asking yourself the "why" questions?

How?

Once we understand, we need to act. For that, we ask the "how" questions. How can I change this situation?

If I can't change the situation, how can I change my role in it so that I'm not affected so much?

How can I change anything I have control of in order to change the situation and my feelings about it?

My example: I couldn't change my Mom, her health issues, or the role it had played in my life. Thankfully, I'd already gotten out of the situation. So in order to change its effect on me, I had to change the only thing I had control over: my mindset and myself.

First, as I told you earlier, these questions helped me change my perspective and the way I saw my Mom. They prompted me to do some research about her illness and get more insight into what her life was really like. An- other thing that may help you do this is to look at a person's background or upbringing.

A lot of times we can be so focused on our own feelings that we forget the others in the situation are people too, with their own issues. I've had other things happen to me that prevented me from seeing someone as a person with feelings because how could a person do that to another person? Right?

But once I became intentional about looking at everyone as a broken person instead of an evil person, it got easier to be compassionate and forgive. It will also help you look at them as an individual and connect whatever happened to who they are, instead of a representation of who you are, what you deserved, or who every person is.

Now this is not to excuse their behavior, or what happened. Not. At. All. We're not justifying anything.

This is to make it easier for you to forgive them, stop blaming yourself, move forward and whatever else will help you begin to heal the wound that you've been covering with a Band-Aid for too long.

Once you're able to disconnect what happened from who you are, it won't change the marks it's left on your life. But it will make the fight for self-worth and confidence easier.

You'll be able to do things to help the pain until it goes away and help yourself believe you're worth being treated as special. You'll fight your feelings of worthlessness by making your mind tell your heart you're enough. Over and over, and over again. And you'll surround yourself with people who will tell you that you're enough when you can't tell yourself.

Then you'll take steps every day to make it easier to believe it's all true.

Those steps are the first six steps of Visible Confidence. But unless you address the roots that make those steps necessary, the fight will become a hard routine instead of a path to healing.

One of my favorite quotes by Muhammad Ali pretty much sums it up:

"I am the greatest. I said that even before I knew I was."

For me, there were a few times I dared to say I was the greatest. But usually, I was just telling myself I was good enough! I was telling myself that I deserved to feel good about myself and to be confident. That I may not have had control over who I'd become up until that point, but that I did have control over who I'd become going forward. After a while of saying it, it all came true.

You tell yourself whatever you want to believe.

Then you do things to make those beliefs easier. Change your mind, move your feet, and your heart will follow.

You may be thinking, "Well Chantelle, I could just do the first six steps in this book without asking all these annoying – and sometimes painful – questions." True, but doing things without understanding the reasons you need to do them keeps all those great results on the surface.

It's like stuffing all the boxes under the bed, table and in the closet instead of unpacking them. As people get closer, they'll eventually uncover something you weren't prepared for.

We want to be confident all the way down to our core. Not scared that someone's going to open a door before we've had time to clean it out.

In the unpacking process, the concept of changing what you can control is important because it does us no good to focus on things we can't. It doesn't mean they're not relevant; it's just not productive.

There may have been other people involved in a situation that hurt you, but you can't change them.

The only thing you can do is address the issue with them and allow that to change something in your own mind and heart. If it also changes them for the better in some way, great! But you can't count on it and let that influence your process.

We can also be tempted to rehash things in our lives that we wish we had done differently. I have plenty of those. But letting memories from the past keep you there is the quickest way to be consumed with guilt and regret.

You can change your location but you can't change the path that brought you there.

Instead of continuing to blame yourself, look at the choices that led you to that place, give yourself some grace and resolve to do things differently the next time you're faced with a similar choice.

Then forgive yourself.

Put all that energy into taking steps forward instead of beating yourself up, so that eventually your mind, heart and body will be where you want them to be.

In my own process, I've had to ask myself each and every one of these questions, and more. What makes it so difficult is having to ask and then listen to what may be painful answers.

I've had to fight through and sometimes argue with the answers I got from my questions, before choosing to move forward with intentional and practical actions as a result.

Healing is not fun but it is necessary.

Your answers will tell you where to look. Start sorting through them. Sometimes it'll involve physically throwing things away. One time I threw away everything that had a certain logo on it so I never had to see it in my closet again.

Or it may involve acknowledging the reason someone made you feel a certain way. Another time, I didn't realize I had a crush on a guy until I sat down and really thought about why something he said made me so angry. You may need to figure out what you're going to do with your own feelings or forgive someone despite an apology you never got.

Other times, it could be a phone call of reconciliation or closure. I've made my share of calls and emails to people asking their forgiveness and clearing the air.

With the deepest wounds, the first step is being conscious of them. What's ignored will never heal so be intentional about getting past your past.

Also, you may need to talk to someone about some of the things that are coming up. There's absolutely nothing wrong with that. We're asking tough questions that are hard to work through alone. Please ask for help during this process if you need it and know that it doesn't make you weak!

That said, there's one more question you need to ask yourself before we move on:

"How does this past hurt show up in my present life?"

Ooh, this one is hard! But the result of a root that's been damaged is fruit that's different than what was meant to grow. It is so important that we figure out what things and characteristics are in our lives simply because of past hurts that we never healed from.

Things happen and they change us. Sometimes they change us a lot. Is this new person really a different person though? Or are you still the same person who has been broken badly enough to stay in survival mode?

Have you found yourself or lost yourself, and how do you know?

The thing about feelings is that no matter how tight we shut the box they're stuffed in, they refuse to stay completely locked away without spilling out into our lives in one way or another.

So who were you before someone hurt you? That person is who you really are. How do you get back to being a smarter, less naïve version of that person? You heal, intentionally, from the ground up.

Get to the root. Make it healthy. Then everything that grows from it will be whole.

My example: Before the situation with my Mom, I was happy, carefree and didn't really question much about myself at all – other than if I was always going to be taller than everyone (laughing). Afterwards, I was angry all the time, started getting into fights and became obsessed with horror movies.

As I got older I began to base my worth on material things and people outside myself. I did a lot of crazy things to make myself feel like enough. But was everything I was doing really who I was? Or was it a manifestation of all the stuff inside that I hadn't dealt with yet?

"Doing bad things doesn't make you a bad girl. It just makes you a good girl, doing bad things."

One of my best friends in high school told me that one time. You are who you are, even if you're acting like someone else. I've completely seen this play out in my own life. As I began to heal, the person I had "found" began to look more and more like the person I was before. I started to feel more like myself than I ever had.

It's crazy because as we use our actions to cope and deal with the pain we're feeling, sometimes they send us father away from who we are. And sometimes it may be other people's actions that help us lose ourselves. Usually it's a combination of both.

No matter how much we've changed or how long we've been in survival mode, we can always, always, *always* heal our way back to the person we were originally meant to be. I see proof of that every day I look in the mirror. It's the entire reason I'm writing this book.

Before you start sorting through your entire head and heart though, hold on a second. If you do it the wrong way, you will not be able to function!

Unpacking is essential to confidence. Doing it on your own time is necessary for success.

When you move, you don't unpack every box and throw everything on the floor, right? You wouldn't be able to walk without falling all over everything. It makes a lot more sense to unpack one box at a time so you can figure out where things go along the way.

Feelings work the same way as you begin to "unpack" them. There's no way you can figure out everything at once. You wouldn't be able to walk around in your life without tripping all over your emotions and dropping every responsibility you're holding on the way down. No, in order to heal with- out letting your life fall apart, it has to be little by little, on your own time.

Don't just open your mind and heart and throw every single thing out into your life.

Sort through one issue, experience or relationship at a time. That way, you'll be able to heal and function without being a complete mess.

For example, in order to still function after a breakup a few years ago, I had to throw all my feelings in a box real quick and get to work on my life. I was moving, changing jobs and it was hectic. I didn't have time to hang out in my house and never get up so I could deal with them.

Once I finally got those feelings to stay in the box, I didn't want to open it, ever. But if you don't figure out how and why something happened, how can you fully heal from it, or prevent it from happening again?

I couldn't just not think about it, or keep doing things to distract myself, or pretend I was over it. I refused to continue on without unpacking because I didn't want to have all of these unresolved issues clouding my judgment of future relationships.

So when enough time had passed to prevent my emotions from crippling me, I opened the box slowly, whenever I had time to myself. I started to actually think about things that would venture through my head instead of pushing them away.

Letting something simply sit on your mind is a powerful way to work through them at first. And whenever those thoughts threatened to take me too low or it was time to function in my life, I'd put them back in the box and start to lose myself in the present again.

Another change I made: Instead of always keeping it together, I let myself cry – still on my own time of course. Don't fall apart at work and then say I told you to. Also, don't let anyone tell you crying doesn't help. Crying helps as long as you use it as a release after which you get up and do something productive.

Now when I see pictures or hear certain songs from that relationship I can smile at the good memories instead of feeling sad that it's over. That's healing and it was intentionally done on my own time.

Keep in mind though, that you already do this. We all have coping mechanisms that we use. You already distract yourself from what you're feeling when you don't want to feel it. You already put things away and live the best you can.

I'm just asking you to be conscious of when you do it and do it with a purpose.

Boxes are meant for moving, not to keep and live with!

No matter how good you are – or become – at compartmentalizing, don't expect everything to be better all at once. Addressing feelings doesn't mean they go away immediately. In fact, you'll probably feel more before you feel less.

At times, inside my head has been the most painful place for me to be. It's also the most productive. One thing that has always helped me is to hang out in my head and heart even when I don't want to, and then to actively and deliberately use what I find there to get better.

You can't clean out a place you never visit.

Don't just visit once; instead, come back often. Unpacking, cleaning and organizing are all things that don't happen overnight.

And so the question always comes up: Who has time for all that? The answer is, "make time."

We all have stuff that we feel is more important in our lives. But sometimes distractions from what you need to be doing come disguised as other things that feel necessary. It all comes back to priorities. Make your development a priority.

About three years ago, I had a small leak in my tire. I knew I needed to get it patched up but I "didn't have time" so I just kept stopping by the gas station and refilling it whenever needed. I totally intended on getting it fixed whenever my schedule allowed...

Until I was driving to a meeting one day and that same tire blew out on the freeway. All of the sudden, finding time wasn't an option. Thank God no one got hurt because of my recklessness, but I still had to call a tow truck, get my car taken to the tire place and buy a whole new tire when I could've just patched the old one. The whole process took about three hours of time I "didn't have."

People are the same way. The best way to be able to live your life at 100% is to intentionally and fully heal after each thing that breaks you, whether it's a small hole that's just an inconvenience, or a blown out tire that threatens to run you off life's freeway.

Do the people you love deserve you at 100%? Are you willing to take the time so that you can live a more confident, full life? Or are you doing just enough maintenance to keep yourself from completely breaking down?

Your growth as a person has to be a priority above everything else. Not in a selfish way but in a practical and loving way. When you don't make time for small things, they turn into big things.

Big things hurt more, take more time to fix and have to be dealt with whenever they happen, as opposed to on your schedule. That means you have to take more time away from the people you love and the other things you're doing instead of taking less time up front.

Don't wait for something to cripple you before you make time to fix it. You may be able to do things without your car but you can't do anything without you!

BONUS CHAPTER
THE NEXT LEVEL – FIND YOUR FAITH

"For we walk by faith not by sight."

This Chapter is about Faith, hence the title (laughing). I actually went back and forth a lot on if I should include it or not.

On one hand, I didn't want to offend anyone and everyone has some sort of feelings about faith. On the other hand, it has made such a huge difference in my life and I know a lot of people do want to hear about it.

So here's the deal. I obviously decided to include it. But if this isn't something you're interested in, I definitely don't want to force it on you.

You already have the 7 Steps to Confidence, which is everything I originally poured into this book, so you can skip right to the conclusion. If you want to.

But if you are interested, I'm excited to have you read a little bit more about the continuation of my personal journey and how I think it can help you.

I spent a lot of time building my confidence from the ground up by doing the things we've talked about so far. It completely changed my life.

Now I can walk into any room with anyone and feel like I have a right to be there. During those moments when I don't necessarily feel like that, I can make myself believe it anyway by doing what I told you to do. Yes, I still use this stuff, all the time. And it still works!

Once I found the path to confidence, I didn't think it got any better than that. I was wrong. There is one thing that will take your Visible Confidence to the next level.

That one thing is FAITH.

The difference between confidence and faith is huge. You can only have confidence in anything you can touch and control.

Like playing a sport, studying for a test or preparing for an interview; the more you practice, the better you get and the better you get, the more confidence you have.

Confidence in the things we can control can always be built. These days, if I can control the situation, I'm confident. I don't care what it is. I feel like if

I'm in it, I'm going to do whatever it takes to make things happen.

But let's be honest with ourselves. There are a lot of things in this world that we can't control. So what happens when we're faced with those things? That's where faith comes in.

Belief in anything we can't control isn't confidence. It's faith.

Faith is the only thing that goes beyond our reach, our vision, the level of our abilities and the abilities of others. It has no limit.

The ceiling of confidence is the floor of faith.

For me this differentiation between confidence and faith is really important. Because even before I practiced my faith, I was showing it in things I couldn't control and calling it confidence. Every time we believe that things will work out the right way or even that we'll wake up with the ability to go out and work hard tomorrow, is faith, not confidence.

Faith is the substance of things hoped for and evidence of what we do not see. ~ Hebrews 11:1

So with faith, if we can't touch it and control it, that means we're trusting something outside of ourselves that's bigger than us to work for our good. Whatever we call that "something" is what we have faith in.

I definitely realize that these days we have a lot of choices in what to call that and what to believe is right. And though I've done a ton of research on a lot of them – I've never been the type to just blindly believe – this chapter isn't going to be an account of all your faith options.

Like I've done throughout this book, I'm just going to tell you what's worked for me.

So when it comes to the "something" I put my faith in, I call Him God, and He's the most important thing in my life, hands down. When the Bible says He loves me and that if I put Him first He'll handle all my needs, I believe it.

Not because of how capable I am or how hard I've worked, but because He's that someone out there who can control and influence the things I can't.

I do what I can do and let Him do what only He can do.

It may sound cheesy and you might not believe it. God knows I didn't! I saw so many people who said they believed in God but didn't have lives I wanted and I was like, "Why would I want to follow you?"

If that's where you are or you've felt like that before, I completely understand. But just hear me out.

What I did in the beginning was blame God for things that other people did in His name, without really getting to know Him for myself. And that wasn't fair. What if I believed everything people ever said about you? Would I know the real you? Probably not, right?

I know you wouldn't know the real me if you believed everything other people ever said. And it's the same with God. He has some of the worst representatives and gossipers ever. But that doesn't mean it's who He is.

And so as I was building my faith, I decided to forget what everyone else said and did, and focus on getting to know Him for myself.

At that point, even though I didn't really believe that this whole God thing worked, there was enough evidence for me to try it. So the first thing I did was to start hanging out with him.

Yep, sounds super simple because it is. You can't trust anyone you don't know and you can't get to know anyone you don't hang out with, even the God of the universe.

Our relationship with Him is just like any other relationship we've ever had in that it takes time and action to go from interest to trust.

If you don't trust Him yet then enough time and effort hasn't been spent.

I think a lot of people mess up by telling us we have to love God right away. I mean, we should totally respect Him for the whole creating the universe thing. But how are we supposed to love someone we don't know?

No, the beginning of our relationship with God starts with us deciding He's interesting enough to learn more about.

It continues with spending time with Him. As you hang out and get to know Him, you'll start to like Him. It'll eventually go from interest to liking to really liking to loving, just like other relationships we're used to.

Trust me, God is ok with that, as long as you're really trying. Jesus didn't tell His first followers to listen to everything He said. He told them to follow Him. Why? Because He knows when we really hang out with Him, we'll love Him eventually!

Hanging out with God means praying and reading the Bible.

Understandably, a lot of people don't want to read the Bible because they don't believe it's true. I was one of those people. I thought the Bible had been written by men and was way too old to have any affect on my life. I mean, a lot has changed in 2,000 years.

But you don't have to believe it's true to read it. Many of Jesus' followers followed Him every day for 3 years thinking He was someone really important without realizing He was actually their Savior. If they can do it, so can we.

You know what'll happen though? After a while, it'll start to make sense. You'll start to feel closer to God and see things differently. I'm telling you, it'll work!

I know it'll work because when I started reading the Bible, it wasn't because I believed it. I just thought, "Maybe God is somewhere in there." I only tried because I wanted to feel closer to Him. And now, He's the best thing ever! (laughing)

What's in it for you?

The Bible can help you do everything we've talked about in this book! Seriously.

1. Chase Fear and Win!

There are a bunch of people in the Bible who were scared to do what God told them to do. Almost everyone He gave an assignment to, actually. Some good examples are Gideon, Esther, Moses, and even Jesus! Yes, they were fearful, everyday people just like you or me.

The cool thing is, the Bible is very honest about their fear. It doesn't paint them as super-human at all. Then we get to see how God came through for them when they ignored their feelings and did what He told them to do anyway!

God told someone not to be afraid at least 365 times in the Bible – enough for every day of the year. And every single time He turned their actions of faith into something greater than they could've ever imagined. Talk about inspiring!

If we believe that's true, then we can also believe God when He says He'll do the same thing for us. All we have to do is follow His lead and use the examples He gives us for encouragement. Thankfully, the Bible talks a lot about overcoming fear... Probably because God knew we would need it!

Find good stuff in: 2 Timothy 1:7, Joshua 1:9, Judges 6:12-16 (Gideon), Esther 4:10-14 (Esther), Exodus 4:10-17 (Moses), Matthew 26:36-46 (Jesus), Isaiah 41:13

2. Look, Feel, Play

The Bible is the ultimate evidence picture because if we believe it, we can believe what it says about us. It says that God loves us, that He made every single thing about us – even the things we hate – on purpose, and that He wants to use us to do amazing things.

According to God, other people's opinions about our beauty don't matter because He has a very different definition of it. He made us beautiful to begin with and if we trust Him, He'll help us to be even more beautiful in His eyes. That's comforting because while people's standard of beauty changes, God's never does.

Since the Bible is the ultimate evidence picture and it tells us how to be beautiful in God's eyes, then Jesus is the best beauty role model ever! That may sound corny but I am corny and it is true.

So yes, when I'm feeling ugly or like I'm not good enough, I do my hair and my make-up and work out and try to help people so that I can have confidence in who I am. But I also pray and read my Bible so that I can have faith that what God says about me is way truer than what I'm feeling at the moment. Faith is so much bigger than confidence!

Find good stuff in: Ephesians 2:10, Psalm 139:13-15, Proverbs 31:30, John 3:30

3. Shine From the Inside

While what we look like can definitely be used to get people's attention – because of how this world works – that's not at all what He cares about. God wants our character to look as much like Jesus as possible. Talk about a high standard!

The cool thing is, the more we hang out with Him, the more we start to talk and act like Him. It's kind of like when your best friend starts using a new word. At first you think it sounds weird and might even make fun of him for it. But then, the more you hear it, the better it sounds.

Suddenly you're saying it and can't remember why it hadn't been part of your vocabulary all along. I know I'm not the only one that's happened to!

That's how hanging out with Jesus is. You will automatically become a better person on the inside and then you'll look back like, "Wow, how did that happen?" Then all the other work you do to get better will be icing on the cake!

Find good stuff in: 1 Corinthians 11:1, Jeremiah 24:7, Romans 12:1-2, Philippians 1:4-6, Psalm 51:10-12

4. Come to Work to Work

You can be driving a hundred miles an hour but if you're facing the wrong direction, you'll never get to where you need to go. That was the story of my life when I first moved to Houston. I couldn't go anywhere without my GPS and there were plenty of times I was running late, speeding in the wrong direction until I could make a U-turn to go in the right one.

In life, God is the best GPS ever! One of my favorite things about following Him is the clarity and direction that comes along with it. The thing is, a lot of roads may look the same when they start but end up taking you to completely different places.

That's where the Bible comes in. It helps us figure out which roads are good choices and which ones just look like they are at the beginning. Working on God's path gives you more direction and purpose. That way, you waste less time and energy on roads that will get you nowhere.

Find good stuff in: Proverbs 6:6-8, Hebrews 12:1-3, 1 Corinthians 9:24-27, Colossians 3:23-24, Proverbs 3:3-8

5. Build Your Team.

The more we know God, the better we'll know us. And the better we know us, the easier it is to be smart about who else we let know us.

The Bible is very clear about which type of people should be in our Inner Circle. When we use that as a guide, relationships get easier, the amount of drama goes down and so does the amount of heartbreak. If those things don't start happening, those people aren't the type of people God was talking about.

Find good stuff in: Romans 12:9-10, John 13:34-35, Hebrews 10:23-25, Galatians 6:1-2, 1 Thessalonians 5:12-14

6. Define The Standard

In my first real relationship, I was treated like a Princess. Pretty awesome, I'd say. It set my expectations high in the love and respect department by teaching me how I was supposed to be treated.

Just like we talked about earlier, once you have a standard for how something is supposed to go, it's a lot harder to settle for less than that. In the love department, we should never have to! The same goes for truly falling in love with God and experiencing His love in return. When that happens, we are so fulfilled and feel so valuable that it's a lot harder for us to allow people to treat us as less than we're worth.

Get to know God and let Him set the standard for the loving relationships in your life. The Bible has a pretty awesome and comprehensive definition of what love is. Plus, where better to get the definition of something than from its creator?

Find good stuff in: 1 John 4:8, 1 Corinthians 13:4-7, Ezekiel 36:24-30, Romans 8:38-39, 1 Chronicles 16:34

7. Unpack Your Experience

The point of asking "why" is so that we can dig inside ourselves and begin to heal our heart. That's the part of us that God cares the most about! Even if our heart is all messy and broken to start with, He promises that if we follow Him, he'll give us a new one!

This is another one of His promises that I've seen come true in my own life. It has been really amazing to hand God all the broken pieces of myself and watch Him put me back together, little by little. I believe that God fixes the Brokens and then sends them out to help other Brokens. I love being used to help Him put some people back together again.

No matter how many questions we ask and how hard we try, God is the only one who can completely heal every hurt. We can heal some, but He heals all.

Just like we'll never get better if we're chronically ill but take our meds once a week, God can't heal us if we don't actually have a relationship with Him, even if we visit on Sundays, Wednesdays or whenever else. He's not going to take the pieces of your heart from you. You have to give them to Him.

Find good stuff in: John 7:37-38, Jeremiah 29:11-14, Isaiah 55:8-11, Hebrews 4:15-16, Psalm 145:17-19, Psalm 34:18

So that's what I believe on the faith side of things. I gave you a lot of reference scriptures above so a great start would be to look them up!

Also, people always ask me where to start reading. Whatever you do, don't start in Genesis! It's a great book but also a great way to kill the beginning of a brand new reading plan.

A great place to start reading in the Bible is the book of John (the fourth book in the New Testament, not the little ones in the back). It's awesome because its writer, John, was super close to Jesus and so he included details about Jesus' feelings that other accounts of His life didn't. If you read the book of John, I promise you'll get a different picture of Jesus than the way many people make Him seem. And who better to tell you about someone than His best friend? Start there and you can always reach out to me on social media or my website with any questions!

"The fruit of that righteousness will be peace; its effect will be quietness and confidence forever." ~ Isaiah 32:17

THE WRAP UP...

"Visible Confidence in who you are
will always be the most stylish thing in your wardrobe."

Well that was fun! I hope you enjoyed reading my thoughts and experiences on Visible Confidence. Most importantly, I hope it gave you some perspective and practical tips to help you in your own confidence journey.

Remember, Visible Confidence is never flashy but is immediately noticeable. It doesn't come off with anything you can take off.

Everyone can see it, but those who equate worth with status, wealth or appearance will never understand it.

Visible Confidence starts inside us and touches every part of our bodies before spilling out onto those around us.

Don't forget the steps to Visible Confidence:
1. Chase Fear and Win
2. Look, Feel, Play
3. Shine From the
4. Inside Come to Work to Work
5. Build Your Team
6. Define the Standard
7. Unpack Your Experience
BONUS: Find your Faith

I'd love to continue the conversation with you, to hear what you've found useful from the book and how you've put these things into practice in your real life!

Send me a message on my website, www.VisibleConfidence.com or on Instagram and Twitter at @MissChantelle. You can even send me your evidence pictures, requests for Bible study tips or other questions! I'll be answering everything.

I'm super excited to hear from you! God bless and until next time, live confidently!

65872452R00058

Made in the USA
Lexington, KY
28 July 2017